MILLIONAIRE AUTHOR

The Busy Entrepreneur's Guide to Writing a Book
Everyone Wants to Read

STEPHANIE J HALE

www.oxfordwriters.com

Copyright

Powerhouse Publications
94/124 London Road,
Oxford
OX3 9FN

Print Edition

British Library Cataloguing in Publication Data.
A catalogue record for this book is available from the British Library.

For my grandparents, Richard and Dorothy Griffin, the first entrepreneurs to inspire and teach me – though I didn't know it at the time

CONTENTS

STEPHANIE J HALE, BEM

*"It's too easy in today's whirlwind world for
books not to get written."*

Stephanie J. Hale is a multiple award-winning author of 11 books, and founder of Oxford Literary Consultancy and Powerhouse Publications.

She's worked with some of the most iconic authors and well-known entrepreneurs alive today. She also loves discovering fresh talent and turning unknown writers into best-selling authors featuring on radio and TV.

She's experienced in negotiating with literary agents and Hollywood film producers, as well as organising book serialisations and giveaways in newspapers and magazines.

She started her career as a BBC and IRN newsreader and journalist, before accepting the prestigious position of Assistant Director of Creative Writing at Oxford University.

She was awarded a British Empire Medal for services to authors by the Queen in 2017.

I was speaking to an Australian entrepreneur recently who told me that he's had a book "burning in my belly since I was a child". There was an ache in his voice and yearning in his eyes. "I won't feel I've fulfilled my life's purpose until it's written," he told me. I reassured him that he could easily get the first draft down if he could set aside half an hour a day for the next two or three weeks. But he shook his head; he doesn't have the time even for that. He's now 58, and has no plans for retiring. I suspect his book may never see the light of day.

It's all too easy in today's whirlwind world for life to take over and books not to get written. You might start by telling yourself that you'll do it when your current business project is finished or when your kids are grown up. Except that your mailbox is always full, your workload seems to get heavier, and eventually you have elderly parents and grandchildren to care for, as well as your children. "I'll do it next year," rolls into next year ... and keeps rolling.

If you are an expert in your field and you want to share your message or help others, then this book is for you. It's especially for you if you feel like you want to write a book, but there just aren't enough hours in the day, and you're starting to despair of ever getting it written. It's also for you if you're quietly wondering whether it'll be worth the time and effort.

If any of this sounds familiar, rest assured that there is hope. As a mother of three and a busy-itis addict myself, I can assure you that it is possible to write a book even when it feels like you have no time. What's more, you can do it in an enjoyable way, fitted around your work and family commitments. I am going to show you how to stop unnecessarily overthinking and overcomplicating the process. I will help you fit it into your schedule, even if you work a 60-hour week or have an insanely busy family life.

What better way to help you, than by asking some of the busiest entrepreneurs on the planet to share their experiences of writing books? These are people who have exactly the same number of hours in the day as you do. If they can find time to write books, with their busy schedules, then anyone can. I know, because helping to bring books to life is what I do each day.

By the end of reading this book, you will be sufficiently inspired and motivated to write your book. You'll have the exact same toolkit that has helped other incredibly busy entrepreneurs. Imagine how it will feel to be able to tick this off on your wish list once and for all.

Is it lack of time that's stopping most people from writing their books, or are there other factors?

This is interesting. Many people have a fixed belief that writing a book is complicated and difficult. They think they can't get it written because they don't have the time. That's not strictly true. But we'll come to that in a moment.

Some of the other top reasons that people tell me why they haven't written their books are these:

- *I have too many ideas and don't know which one to pick.*
- *I don't know enough to fill an entire book.*
- *I don't know where to get started.*
- *What if no one reads it?*
- *What if I can't get it published?*
- *I don't know what to keep in and what to leave out.*
- *I have small children.*
- *There's no money in books.*
- *Someone else wrote a book similar to mine.*
- *I need to do more research.*
- *I'm just not feeling inspired.*
- *I pitched my idea to publishers, but no one liked it.*
- *I don't know how to structure it.*
- *What if it's no good?*

You'll see from this list that it's not really a lack of time that's preventing most people from writing a book. Mindset plays a massive part – especially if you are held back by self-doubt or perfectionism.

Let me illustrate this in a somewhat dramatic fashion: if your children were kidnapped and the ransom was to produce a book within seven days, could you do it? You already know the answer. So the reality is that it's more about having a *big enough incentive* to write your book.

I work with incredibly busy professionals at the top of their game, who sometimes seem to have barely enough time to sneeze, let alone write a book. Often, they speak to me on their car phones en route to meetings. Some Skype me in their pyjamas, several hours before most people are even awake. I've had clients call me while sitting on airplanes waiting for take-off. I've even had one call me between contractions while in the early stages of labour! These are high octane, high achievers with more responsibilities than they know what to do with. Yet interestingly, they still find time to write books. I am going to show you how.

I often have entrepreneurs come to me wanting to write and publish a book in time for a conference they're speaking at. I'll ask, "What's your deadline?" and they'll reply, "Yesterday." Recently, for example, I had a corporate finance expert call me – he'd somewhat recklessly announced to everyone at a business networking meeting that he'd written a book! He came away from that event with 30 leads for his consultancy and six new clients. But he was also in a panic, as he'd only written five pages and a jacket blurb! We got the first draft of his book written in under 12 hours after we had plotted it out. Then, he spent a week editing and rewriting it. It's remarkable what can be achieved when you have sufficient motivation.

You mentioned there is a misconception about why people don't write their books. Can you explain more?

Let me start by stressing that I'm talking about non-fiction books here. Novels are a different matter altogether.

The main reason is that most people try to write what I call their "legacy book" first. A legacy book contains every little last drop of their wisdom. So they are often trying to take 10, 20, 30 or more years of knowledge and squeeze it all into their very first book. They are still inexperienced at book writing, but they choose a complex book, rather than starting with a simpler, easier format. This is like taking the contents of a four-drawer filing cabinet, then trying to cram it all into an A4 envelope. This is overwhelming for most people, even if they are experts at the top of their field. They find it too much of a struggle and eventually give up.

Another reason is that most aspiring authors try to write their book by hand, or type it, when they may actually be more suited to speaking. The average speed for most of us when we type is around 40 words per minute – or, optimistically assuming that your fingers won't pause, 2,800 words per hour. When you speak, you're likely to have a speed of 150 words per minute. So it's almost four times faster to dictate a book than it is to type it. It's also much easier on your finger joints!

Most experts talk about their specialist subject all day long. They talk about it to clients, to customers, to colleagues, to friends. They may even host seminars or lecture at conferences and expos. It never occurs to them to use the dictation app on their phone or computer. They have a fixed conception in their mind about how an author *should* write and how a book *should* be written, so they make the process way more complicated than it needs to be. They may also feel like they need to do a ton of research when in fact everything they need is right there in their head just waiting to be tapped into.

When it comes to structure, there is a general misconception about what a non-fiction book should look like. This is usually the conventional linear plotline, backed up with research and perhaps charts and data. Again, the thought of gathering lots of information and putting it into a logical order feels too daunting a task for most people. This ignores the fact that many non-fiction readers read books in a non-linear fashion, dipping in and out, and skipping topics that aren't relevant to them. It's a very different experience compared with reading a novel, where if you miss the opening chapter you won't have a clue what's happening later in the story.

Similarly, some first-time authors may feel the need to add quotes and extracts from other books and authors to back up their arguments. These extracts then need copyright approval from publishers' permissions departments, which can be a lengthy – and sometimes, expensive – process. It never occurs to them to reword and repurpose the quotations using their own words. I'm not talking about plagiarism here, more about using the quotes as inspiration for your own ideas.

To give you an example of how this might work: "The pen is mightier than the sword" is a well-known adage, coined by English playwright, Edward Bulwer-Lytton. If I wanted to use this at the start of my book, I could easily echo the sentiment, by writing: *"Your pen is the most powerful weapon for changing the world" – Stephanie J Hale.* The original quote is from an 1839 play so there's no copyright issue to worry about, and my version is a little clumsy, but hopefully you get the idea. This technique neatly positions you as an authority in your own right, rather than putting you in a deferential position to another expert – and often, unintentionally, giving a free advert for rival services.

Ironically, most of us understand the concept of deadlines in our work. We usually have a clear goal or objective that is broken down into smaller targets that fit into our schedule. If we didn't do this, we wouldn't get paid. Yet very few people seem to use the same principle when it comes to writing a book. They don't map out their book. They don't set themselves targets. Instead, they write when the whim takes them or when they feel they can fit it in. Imagine if you took the same approach with your clients and customers: "I know I promised to have x ready for you by today. But I just didn't feel in the mood." "When will you finish it?" "Erm, I'm not sure. Maybe next year or perhaps the year after that..." There's a lot to be said for treating your book as a business project rather than a creative endeavour.

Many aspiring authors overthink their book rather than just getting it written. They want everything to be perfect. So they might try to edit their book as they write, polishing and polishing each chapter before they move on to the next. This not only slows the progress of the first draft, but often takes the life and energy out of a book before it's even had the chance to get going. The plot loses momentum, and they progressively lose their enthusiasm. I'm a big advocate of getting down your first draft before you even consider going back to the beginning and re-reading it.

Finally, and most crucial of all: your book needs to be at the top of your to-do list, rather than floating around at the bottom. If you hope to do it in your spare time, it's unlikely to happen. You need to give yourself a clear intention of finishing it by a fixed date. Block out time in your diary to get it written, even if it's just for 30 minutes per day spread over several weeks. I had one client, who was a property investor working 14-hour shifts, who wrote her book on the Tube on her way to work each day. There is no question her dedication paid off, as she ended up being asked to feature in a programme on Channel 5 after her book was published; she also appeared in *Radio Times* magazine.

What are your top tips to get a book written when you're pressed for time?

The first question to ask yourself is: can you set your "legacy" book aside for the time being? Is there an easier book you can write? (I'll make some suggestions for simpler books in a moment.)

You may also find it easier if you make your book more about your readers and less about you:

- Who is your ideal reader?
- What are their biggest problems and challenges?
- What are their biggest dreams and aspirations?
- What is important to them?
- What is it that they most want to know?
- What value can you give them?

I find that many people, even those who are famous and successful, feel vulnerable when it comes to writing a book. I can think of a client who is a Radio 4 presenter, for example, who told me on the day of his book launch: "This is the most terrifying day of my life!" Authors often feel like they are putting their reputation on the line. They worry what their family will think. They fear that their peers will judge them. They don't want to get it wrong or look stupid. So by placing the emphasis more on your reader, and thinking what they most want and need to read about, it takes your ego out of the equation. This should enable you to write without hearing the critical voices in your head.

I also suggest that you think about your book length. You are likely to have more flexibility with this if you are self-publishing or approaching a small indie publisher. Do you really need to write 90,000 words for your first book? Or can you write a smaller book of 30,000 or 40,000 words? Do you have to write a text-heavy book, or can you write a book that has more photos or pictures?

Don't be afraid to use your imagination and creativity when it comes to planning your book. Can you structure it in a less traditional way? I am by profession a newsreader and journalist, so it feels very natural for me to ask questions and interview people for example, hence the format of this book.

Other examples might be:

- A book with lots of photos and less text.
- A book with lots of graphics and "white space".
- A collection of essays from experts in your field.
- Contributor chapters from colleagues or clients.
- 25 FAQs in your area of expertise.
- Top tips from your staff.
- Funny anecdotes from clients or customers.
- Top mistakes to avoid.
- A recipe book.
- A book of inspirational quotes.
- A diary, journal, or workbook with your logo and branding.
- Client case studies.
- A step-by-step how-to guide in words or pictures.
- A "day in the life of" or "week in the life of" showcase of your work.
- A series of brief books on different aspects of your business.
- A workbook, with practical exercises and space to jot down light bulb moments.

I recently worked with a businesswoman who asked her six staff to each write a chapter for her book. This was great for generating a feel-good factor with her team and gave them an opportunity to be co-authors when they wouldn't otherwise have written books of their own.

Initially, you may feel resistant to the idea of speaking your book into voice recognition software or a Dictaphone. I know I certainly was – it seemed wrong somehow to write a book by speaking it; it wasn't "proper writing". We all have a culturally ingrained idea of how things should be, usually given to us while studying English at school (think, William Shakespeare with quill in hand). No doubt, the first generation of writers to use manual typewriters felt something similar when switching from pen and ink. When you think about it logically, it's still your words and ideas, just a different method for getting them onto the page.

It may take a couple of hours to learn to use the dictation software. You need to enunciate slowly and clearly, and resist the temptation to edit as the words appear on your computer screen. But it's a skill worth mastering as it will revolutionise the way you manage your time. You can use this for emails and business letters too and you'll be amazed how much extra time it gives you back each week.

Once you've decided how you are going to write your book, it becomes a matter of simple mathematics. If you speak for 60 minutes and record it, you should have around 9,000 words. If you want to write a 70,000-word book, you'll therefore need to block out around 60 minutes per day over 10 days in your diary. For this, I recommend adding a couple of extra days to allow for false starts and deletions. If you want to write a 35,000-word book, you can halve this. Just block out the time in your schedule, and make it part of your daily routine. You can write a list of questions yourself and go through answering them. Or you may find it beneficial to ask a colleague to interview you to keep you on track and stop you going off on a tangent.

I have a couple of clients who have achieved this over the space of a weekend. It was exhausting, and they had sore throats by the end of it. But if you're pushed for time, it can certainly be done.

All that's left is to commit to it. Tell as many people as you can that you're writing a book. Put a post on Facebook, Twitter or LinkedIn. Tell your family, friends, and clients. Give yourself accountability so that there will be a loss of face if you don't achieve it.

I recently spoke at a business seminar where one of the attendees, the owner of a film production company, was so motivated by my talk that he stood up and announced he was going to write the first draft of his book before the next meeting. It was such a brave and confident thing to do, that I came away certain that he'd achieve it.

Is it worth the time and effort?

Everyone has a different reason for writing a book. Some of them are big change-the-world reasons. Others are more personal and poignant, such as paying tribute to a loved one or drawing attention to an injustice. Maybe you've recovered from a life-changing event and want to share what you've learned.

Many entrepreneurs use a book as a lead magnet to attract new clients. They give books away to answer frequently asked questions, which leverages their time and filters out time wasters. They also multipurpose their book as a ring-bound manual or downloadable MP3, so that it helps both staff and clients.

It can be very lucrative to give books away as free gifts too. One client I work with, who runs a large property company, told me it's no-brainer for him to give away over 3,000 books each year, as he gains over £1 million in new clients.

Here are some of the top reasons why people say they want to write a book:

- *I want to educate others and share my knowledge.*
- *It'll position me as an authority and go-to expert.*
- *I want to stand out from my competitors.*
- *It'll attract new clients and customers.*
- *It will give me a global audience.*
- *I want to expose a myth or misconception.*
- *I want to be featured by newspapers, magazines, and radio.*
- *It's a great "business card".*
- *I want to write a best seller.*
- *I want to win literary awards.*
- *I want TV and movie opportunities.*
- *It'll give me joint venture and sponsorship opportunities.*
- *It's a handbook and operations manual for staff.*
- *It'll be a fantastic free giveaway.*
- *It will add extra value to seminars and workshops.*
- *It'll raise my profile for big corporates.*
- *It'll give me more speaking opportunities.*
- *It'll be a memorable gift for clients and colleagues.*
- *I want to write it for my children and grandchildren.*
- *I want to raise money for charity.*

I'm sure you can relate to one or two of these reasons, and perhaps even add a few of your own.

If you want to elevate your business to the next level, there's no doubt that a book can achieve this for you. Little gives me more pleasure than seeing a new client come to me full of self-doubt and uncertainty about their book idea, then helping them to turn it into an award-winning book with global media coverage. A couple of years ago, I worked with a relationship expert on her first book. She was consumed with doubts the entire time she was writing it, but she went on to win six much-deserved literary awards, as well as becoming a go-to expert for *The Daily Mail*. Many writers aren't good at blowing their own trumpet, so sometimes I have to do it for them!

What about quality?

Is there any qualitative difference between a book that's taken three years to write and one that's been written in three days? Surprisingly, not always. I've read many a badly-written book where the poor author has slogged over it and poured their heart and soul into it (I can think of a judge who handed me a manuscript that read like something written by a 12-year-old, after labouring on it for seven years). I've also read many awe-inspiring and brilliant books, written in just hours, that have either haunted or wowed me.

I was recently working with a horse whisperer who showed me chapters for her book that she'd polished "20 or 30 times" over the years. She then showed me a chapter she'd dashed out for me only the night before. She was shocked when I told her that the unpolished chapter was just as powerful. But it freed her up to finally finish her book, and she's since secured a publishing deal with a small indie press.

Should I tell my personal story?

I'm often asked: "Should I write a how-to book or more of a memoir?"

Most readers are motivated to buy non-fiction books because they have a problem they want to solve. Sometimes pleasure, or passion for a topic, can prompt them too. But more often, it's pain – and getting rid of it – that is the biggest motivator.

A memoir is very difficult to sell (even if you have an extraordinary story) unless you're a well-known celebrity. A book that solves a problem is always going to be easier to promote and sell. However, it's difficult to create a truly unique and original book, as most topics have already been written about.

For this reason, it can be a great idea to blend the two elements to give your book a bit of extra zing! This enables the reader to learn from your lessons and to simultaneously feel as if they've made an emotional connection with you. I recently worked on a litigation book, for example, which might otherwise have been a dry and boring subject – except that the author blended legal facts with the poignant story of how she was orphaned as a baby in Zimbabwe, and how she watched her mother struggling to raise eight children on her own. The book brings tears to your eyes when you are least expecting it.

People tend to buy a book with their heart rather than their head, especially if it strikes an emotional chord. They are much more likely to resonate with a personal account than an academic textbook. So think about the way your book will make your readers feel – whether happy, sad, hopeful, or inspired. Do you want your readers to read your book because they feel they *ought* to, or because they can't put it down?

I'm not good at English – does that matter?

I've taught creative writing students at both Oxford and Cambridge University. I've also held writing workshops for inmates in several prisons in Oxfordshire and Buckinghamshire. The university students were proficient in English grammar, literary conceits, and linguistic flourishes. In comparison, some of the inmates were illiterate and could barely spell. However, it was the *stories* that captured my attention every time, rather than an aptitude for the English language.

There's a lot of snobbery and elitism surrounding books in literary circles and academia. Indeed, there's a whole business model that's grown up around studying to write a book, and taking two or three years to do it. So I know some people will find my views controversial. But ultimately, it's storytelling and the ability to spin a good yarn that sells books, not beautiful grammar. Poor punctuation can usually be fixed by a proofreader or editor, but lack of life experience can't! What matters more is your ability to capture the imagination, to arouse curiosity, to help people, and to hold their attention. I've yet to hear anyone say: "I loved *War & Peace*. Don't you just love the way Tolstoy uses semicolons?"

Similarly, I've noticed that many people tend to 'orate' when they write a book – as if they are standing at a lectern at the front of a lecture theatre. They write how they feel an author ought to write: in a slightly stilted, formal style, rather than in an authentic manner. This adds extra stresses to the process of writing, as the voice isn't naturally their own. It is far better to write in a relaxed and informal way as if you are speaking intimately to a friend.

What do you think about hiring a ghostwriter?

Should you use a ghostwriter or should you write a book yourself? I think ghost-writing is an unnecessary expense in most cases unless perhaps English is your second language. It's usually more satisfying for you to tell your own story in your own words. But if your back's against the wall, and your lack of time has got so bad that your choice is a ghost-written book or no book at all, then this may be your best option.

Most ghostwriters sign a non-disclosure agreement forbidding them from revealing their involvement in a book; they risk a lawsuit if they breach this. Their name will never be on your book cover unless you choose to give them credit. So, it should stay as a confidential arrangement between the two of you.

If you're opting for a ghostwriter, pick a good one. I can think of a restaurateur who hired a cheap copywriter online to write his e-book, but it was a false economy as it was so badly written. The best ghostwriters will mimic your voice so perfectly that even your family shouldn't be able to tell the difference.

Due diligence can be tricky as most ghostwriters are prevented from revealing the names of the books they've written – and if they do breach confidentiality and reveal the titles, then would you really want to work with them? It's therefore best to ask them to write a couple of sample chapters before committing to an entire book and to keep regular checks on their progress.

You'll still need to set aside time to brief them, read what they've written, ask for corrections, and manage the project. So you may decide ultimately that it's easier to write your book yourself.

Should I use illustrations?

A picture speaks a thousand words, as they say. Illustrations can alter the tone of a book and lighten up an otherwise weighty message. I strongly urge you to resist the temptation to allow your friends or family to do this for you – even if they're professional photographers or illustrators. In my experience, this usually leads to problems of one sort or another. Often, authors become so emotionally attached to the image that they can't see that it's sending out totally the wrong marketing message for their book.

These days, it's incredibly easy to find and commission high-quality artists, cartoonists, and illustrators using the Internet. Just ask them to create a couple of sample illustrations first to make sure you're both on the same wavelength.

Many years ago, I was involved in a project where a well-known artist, who had worked for Richard Branson, was commissioned to produce illustrations for a fiction book. His style was wonderful for corporate functions or celebrity parties, but to my mind was a mismatch with the topic and cover of the book. Different styles and genres don't always mix, though you may not realise it until after the work is complete.

You can also buy professional digital images and graphics from various photo libraries online. Make sure you buy the right size images – the resolution needs to be at least 300 dpi – otherwise, they will look pixilated or blurry around the edges when your book is published.

Can I write about people I know without getting sued?

Case studies and real-life anecdotes can be a wonderful way of showcasing the transformations that happen in people's lives. It makes a book feel applicable and real, rather than conceptual and abstract. However, you do need to consider and bear in mind Libel and Privacy Laws.

You can write about real-life situations in a number of ways.

The first is to use case studies with the person's agreement and permission. You can ask them to sign a legal agreement and financial waiver after showing them what you have written. Or if you prefer, you can pay them a small fee or offer another incentive, such as a donation to their favourite charity.

Alternatively, you can disguise real identities by changing gender, appearance, profession, and geographic location, so that people can't be recognised, even by themselves.

Another technique is to invent fictional characters to illustrate your points. These might be caricatures, animals, or fun cartoon figures that lighten up an otherwise solemn message. (Think *Who Moved My Cheese?* and *Eat That Frog.)*

All of these methods are vivid because they dramatise events and *show* your reader what you are talking about. They make your message tangible and believable. They give your reader situations they can relate to, rather than feeling like they are receiving a lecture from a podium.

If you do decide to write about real-life people and events, I recommend booking a brief consultation with a media lawyer to make sure you're on the right side of the law. This will save you potential headaches later on. Just because something is "true" doesn't always mean you can write about it. You need to be able to *prove* that it is true, have convincing witness testimonials, and be able to convince a judge in a court of law that your intentions are non-malicious.

(I offer a free report "How to Write About People You Know Without Getting Sued" to give general guidelines. Please contact me via my website **www.oxfordwriters.com** if you'd like a copy.)

How important is your book title?

Imagine yourself on Amazon looking for a book. First, you tap keywords into the search bar. Then, you skim down the page looking at the titles and glancing at book covers.

It's a three-second decision. If something catches your eye, you click on the link and read the blurb. If it doesn't, then you're straight on to the next page. This is why it's not just important to have an attention-grabbing title, but a catchy and relevant subtitle too. The Internet has reduced people's attention span and their patience levels. This is the Now Culture and most professional authors realise that they have to cater to it.

So beware of getting too attached to your book title unless you've done your market research and tested it on your potential readers. A good title needs to succinctly summarise and encapsulate what your book is about while arousing curiosity at the same time. If you make it too obscure or clever-clever, people won't get it. It'll be more a case of "Whaaat?" than "Wow!"

How do I know if my book idea is strong enough?

Get feedback. Many people get a little shy and embarrassed while talking about their books. They often work in secret and don't even show their parents or partners what they're writing. Maybe it's a throwback to being in the classroom at school, but even confident people suddenly seem to become coy or self-conscious.

However, for the sake of your book it's essential to be open to criticism, to welcome it, and to use it to improve your writing – even if it's not always what you want to hear. If you don't, silly mistakes and errors can slip through. For example, I spoke to a buy-to-let entrepreneur recently who had named one of his book chapters, "The Oldest Profession" (referring to "bricks and mortar") without considering that most people tend to associate that phrase with prostitution. I had another author who had a tendency to keep saying, "To tell the truth." He was aiming to build trust and credibility – but what's the first thing you think when you hear that phrase? Too often, I see manuscripts with "Foreword" spelled as "Forward" right at the front of their book.

Unless you get a book checked, silly mistakes can fall through the net and make you look incompetent. It's therefore vital to ask for frank and honest feedback before a book is launched. If you don't want to show it to your friends, there are great editors available who are skilled at finding your blind spots and giving constructive feedback to make your book more marketable.

What do I do with my book when it's finished?

You have two choices when a book is finished. You can take the traditional route and pitch your book to a literary agent or publisher. Or, you can self-publish. There is no one-size-fits-all solution. The answer is different for everybody depending on your skill set.

In the past, self-publishing was looked down on a little snootily, and considered as being akin to vanity publishing. However, there have been so many runaway success stories in self-publishing that this is no longer the case. A couple of weeks ago, one of my clients ran a promotion for his very first e-book (a psychological thriller) which was downloaded by more than 50,000 readers over 24 hours. Another of my clients sold over 7 million copies of his self-published novels all by himself, with little marketing, and thought he'd "done something wrong" when he sold 28,000 copies with his most recent book. In comparison, many mainstream publishers start with a print run of 3,000 copies and are happy if they achieve these sales!

It is a common misconception that a publisher will do all of your marketing for you. You will usually do the lion's share of marketing in return for 10% royalties on sales. However, if you are hoping to sell a movie option or have your book translated in multiple countries, then securing a literary agent and a mainstream book deal can work in your favour.

Print-on-demand publishing (PoD) – whereby one book is printed when one book is ordered – has created a wonderful opportunity for new authors. You no longer have to pay thousands of pounds for a bulk print run and have 5,000 paperbacks in your garden shed. You no longer need to stand in a post office queue and package books up for buyers. All this is automated for you, reaching readers around the world, 24/7. Your book can be published in hours or days, rather than waiting up to a year with a traditional publisher. Entrepreneurs, who have an understanding of promotion and marketing, often seem to do better than many traditional publishers.

Back in the day, a first-time author felt almost pathetically grateful if they attracted a bite from a mainstream publisher or a literary agent. They hardly dared to raise a squeak of protest at the often unreasonable clauses in their publishing contract. A traditional book deal was the only way to get into bookstores and attract journalists' attention. Nowadays, most people buy books online, so distribution to bookshops is less of an issue. Authors have multiple choices and options available to them. So self-publishing has given them back their mojo.

Is it really this simple? There must be more to it than this.

You can certainly make writing a book complicated and time-consuming if you wish. You can pick a topic that requires lots of reading and research. You can use a lot of facts, figures, and statistics that need verifying. You can create a complex structure, with sub-plots and sub-sub-plots. You can use quotes that need permissions from publishers or the media. You can write and rewrite, then rewrite your prose again. You can overload your book with symbolism, imagery, and literary allusions. These are just a handful of the many ways that authors make books complicated.

Alternatively, you can harness the talents that you already possess. You can write about a subject that's close to your heart that you talk about every day. You can use reports, talks, or blogs that you've already written. Or you can even get your clients, staff, or colleagues to contribute and help you write your book.

I've summarised each chapter of this book with bullet points for you to read if you're super busy, so you really have no excuses. Try it. What have you got to lose?

You've written 11 books to date. Why do you keep writing them?

Like most entrepreneurs, I've had my fair share of ups and downs, both with my health and my personal life. At one of my lowest points, I was living in a refuge with my son, who was about three at the time. I spent several years as a single mother in properties with toadstools on the walls, mould on the furniture, and with water pouring in through the ceiling.

Ironically, that experience – and other challenges that followed – changed my life in many positive ways and made me the person I am today. It's been important for me to share what I learned in those years: that it's possible to bounce back from adversity if you adopt a can-do attitude and focus on your blessings rather than your challenges. This is the underlying theme for most of my books and is what inspires and motivates me.

Books help you to reach out to people all over the world – they have transformed my life and those of my clients. It still gives me a thrill when I see an author getting awards or a TV interview for a book I've helped them with. When they've wrestled with self-doubt and told me, "I'm not sure anyone will want to read it," it gives me even more satisfaction when they're in the spotlight and everyone is singing their praises. I just can't help saying to them: "See, I was right. I told you so!" That gives me such a buzz.

How did Oxford Literary Consultancy come about?

I'm a journalist by profession — my first article was published in a newspaper when I was 15 and I got my first front-page splash when I was 20. I then moved into radio and television as a reporter and newsreader for IRN and the BBC, as well as a flagship radio station launched by celebrity, Bruno Brookes. I loved news reading, but I also wanted to write books, so I used to get up at 4am to write before I went to work or I'd squeeze in the time on weekends when everyone else was out partying.

Eventually, it dawned on me that books were where my real passion lay, so I applied for an MA in Creative Writing with the late Malcolm Bradbury and Whitbread winner Rose Tremain. They rejected me the first time, but accepted me the second time I applied. I got a literary agent and my first book deal off the back of that.

I was offered a really great TV job after I finished that course, but I turned it down as I realised it wouldn't allow me time to write. Instead, I followed my heart, took a whopping pay cut, and became literature development officer for Buckinghamshire, where I was organising literary festivals, and bringing creative writing into prisons and schools. After this, I started lecturing at various colleges within Oxford University, and I was eventually invited to become Assistant Director of Creative Writing, which I enjoyed for several years.

I think I had two books published by this stage, and I'd won a few literary awards. Over the years, people kept asking for my advice about writing books and getting published, so it felt like a natural progression to set up my own literary consultancy. I never expected it to be as successful as it's been. I've gone from working on my own at my kitchen table with a handful of clients, to having a database of over 25,000 and having a team of over 100 editors, proof-readers, typesetters and designers to help me.

I've worked with pretty much every genre you can think of over the years and, as books are usually based on authors' private lives, I've been a confidante to the secrets of many people in the public eye. I've also seen a great many writers go from relatively unknown to supernova – Philip Pullman (author of *His Dark Materials* trilogy) and Jacqueline Wilson (*Tracy Beaker* series) in particular spring to mind, as when I first hired them to speak at my events not many people had heard of them and they had very small audiences. Now, of course, it's a totally different story! First-time authors sometimes forget that even the big names were once unknown. As Mark Haddon, author of *The Curious Incident of the Dog in the Night-Time*, once joked to me: "You knew me before I became *Mark Haddon*." I think this sums it up quite nicely.

Most authors are a bit snow-blind when I first meet them, even the experienced ones. They've been so involved in their books, that they can't see their own strengths and weaknesses. My skill is being able to stand back and give frank and honest criticism about their book and how to improve it to make it more marketable. Sometimes it's relatively easy. But when a book is badly written, it's much harder to break the news. I'm often asked if I would ever lie to save an author's feelings. But that would help no one. So I might think carefully about how I phrase things to soften the blow, but I'm always truthful.

Along the way, I have learned so much from the books written and the people who write them. This month, from one of my more unusual books, I've learned a lot about ancient fishing rods kept in bank vaults, which are apparently selling to collectors for up to £100,000. I had no idea such collectors existed up until a few weeks ago! My work is fascinating, and so much fun. That for me is true success.

Summary for Super-Busy Entrepreneurs

- It isn't lack of time that's stopping most people from writing their books. It's usually that they don't have a big enough incentive.
- Don't try to write your "legacy book" that contains every last drop of your wisdom first. Choose a simpler book to start with.
- Consider dictating your book instead of typing it. You'll get the first draft down in under 10 hours.
- Avoid writing a book that needs research, analysis, charts, and data. Write a book using information that's already in your head.
- Avoid using quotes and extracts from other books that then need copyright permission. Consider re-appropriating the quotes as if they are your own.
- Treat your book as a business. Set a clear deadline and then break this down into smaller targets that can be fitted into your schedule.
- Don't edit and re-edit your book as you write it. Wait until you have finished the first draft or you're likely to lose momentum and enthusiasm.
- Set a date by which you will finish your book and then block out writing time in your diary. Allow nothing else to interfere with this.
- Make your book more about your reader and less about you. Ask yourself what they most want to hear and what are the biggest takeaways you can give them?
- Consider if you really need to write a 90,000-word book, or if it can be shorter.

- Consider less traditional ways to structure your book, other than conventional linear prose.

- Ask a friend or colleague to interview you to keep you on track and help you avoid going off on a tangent.

- Give yourself accountability. Tell as many people as you can that you're writing a book so you'll lose face if you don't.

- Consider multipurposing your book as a ring-bound manual or a downloadable MP3.

- Autobiographies and memoirs are difficult to sell unless you're a celebrity. But a how-to book, combined with personal anecdotes, can be very memorable.

- People buy with their hearts rather than their heads, so connect with their emotions.

- Storytelling, and the ability to spin a good yarn, sell books. Poor grammar can be fixed, so don't get too hung up on it.

- Don't write your book as if you are standing at a lectern orating to an audience. Aim for a more relaxed tone, as if you're talking to a close friend.

- Ghost-writing is an option if you have zero time to write a book. Bear in mind, you'll still need to find time to oversee the project.

- Use illustrations or images to lighten the tone of your book, but resist the temptation to allow friends and family to provide pictures.

- Case studies can be a wonderful way of bringing your story to life. However, do bear in mind libel and privacy laws.

- You can ask for written permission to use a real-life story. You can disguise real-life characters' names and identities. Or, you can invent fictional characters.

- Pick a book title and subtitle that are attention-grabbing, but not too obscure.
- Welcome frank and honest criticism of your book – even if it's not what you want to hear. This prevents silly mistakes from slipping through.
- Weigh up the pros and cons of both traditional publishing and self-publishing, as well as your own skills, before deciding on your best option.
- It is a common misconception that a publisher will do all of your book marketing for you. You will usually do the lion's share of promotion in return for 10% royalties on sales.
- If you are hoping to sell a movie option, or have your book translated into multiple languages, securing a literary agent can work in your favour.
- Print-on-demand publishing means that you no longer have to pay an extortionate sum and have 5,000 copies of your book sitting in your attic.

PETER HARGREAVES, CBE

"I wrote my book when I was at my busiest –
during the float."

Peter Hargreaves, CBE, is co-founder of one of the UK's largest investment brokerages, Hargreaves Lansdown.

He built the business with a friend from the spare bedroom in his flat in Bristol in 1981. Peter spotted a gap in the market and realised that by using newsletters he could give investment fund recommendations to savers and investors.

Hargreaves Lansdown now has over 700,000 customers and manages £70 billion worth of savings, pensions, and investments.

The firm floated with a price tag of £800 million in 2007, and Peter stood down as Chief Executive in 2010.

Peter is known to be modest in his expenditure and doesn't own racing cars, yachts or foreign property. He believes he is the only person to have ever founded a FTSE 100 company without borrowing a penny.

He is author of *In for a Penny: A Business Adventure*, published in 2009.

What inspired me to write my book in the first place was a chap called Jack Bourne. He was quite a character, and he was a real oldster in the industry. He worked for the famous Schlesinger team, who were fantastic at selling funds if performance wasn't as good, and eventually, he worked for Abbey Life's unit trust department. I remember him coming to me one day and saying, "I'm going to come and see you three more times, Peter..." because I think I was a bachelor at the time, it was a long time ago. He said, "I'm going to come and see you when you get married; I'm going to come and see you when you're a millionaire, and I'm also going to come and see you when you write your first book." So it was in my mind.

I am absolutely diabolical at spelling, though over the years I realized that I am a good storyteller. I've told so many good stories, even just in our newsletter. So I thought, "I bet I could write a book," and of course, you always do things like this when you're busy. So I wrote my book when I was at my busiest – during the float.

So you wrote your book during the float of Hargreaves Lansdown. Why did you choose to do it at such a busy time? How did you find the time?

Because I think your brain's racing. You're absolutely at full throttle, aren't you? I was on the ceiling with excitement, and these were good times for the business as well. The market had been good for two or three years, and everything was running really well. Of course, you become very enthusiastic and excited. So I wrote the book during the float in probably six weeks. I used a Dictaphone.

So you dictated your book. You weren't ever tempted to use a ghostwriter?

Oh God, no. I don't think anyone could tell the story as well as me, and all the people that know me well can "hear" me in the book. I don't think a ghostwriter could ever put that into it.

I did get the book edited. My editor, he did drop a few things out, which I thought were very good. So I got him to put them back. Because I said, "Look, it's my book." And he replied, "Well, I don't think it's a particularly good point." To which I said, "I think it's a fantastic point. Put it back." So I had the final word.

The opening of the book is quite attention-grabbing, with the three-card trick where you were ripped off in Times Square. Did you have to think much about how you were going to start your book or was that just the obvious anecdote?

Well, when that happened I was in New York with a chap called John Stone, who also appears in the book at a later stage. He's quite a character.

That evening, we went out for dinner somewhere. We always had a beer or a cocktail before we went out, in the hotel we were staying in. I announced to a few people what had happened, and John Stone was astounded that I actually told them I'd been ripped off. He said, "I can't believe you told that story!" I said, "Well, actually, I thought it was a good lesson for everyone," and I'm not that embarrassed about it. I think you should always make everything into a lesson, and the lesson here was: when something looks too good to be true, it almost certainly is. So I just thought it was a nice start because it was rather self-deprecating as well. And the book is a little bit that way, isn't it?

Yes, there are a lot of personal anecdotes in the book. For example, you mention the lessons you learned from your dad at the bakehouse. You also mention the time when you were asked to give a speech about "change" at school. Though you talked about money "change" rather than the other kind of change!

I didn't remember that myself – it was a very old pal of mine that remembered and reminded me about it. When I go up north and see all my old pals, they're just the same. They make no fuss. They won't allow me to buy more rounds than my share. And you know, it's just: "Alright, Pete. Good to see you again." No fuss. Because they're real mates, you see.

There must have been so many anecdotes you wanted to include in your book: how did you decide what to keep in, and what to leave out?

I wrote most of it from memory. I've never kept a diary, so basically, that was all I could remember at the time. I've thought of other things since, which I possibly could have put in. The only thing that helped me a little bit is that I had all the back-copies of the Hargreaves Lansdown newsletter, which was quite a help. So that helped keep me on track; as I went through them, I kept remembering the various things we did.

So that served as an *aide memoir* to help you remember bits and pieces. Did you use post-it notes, or bullet points, or anything like that to guide you?

I think there was a timeline for part of the book, obviously. The bit about investment in the middle, which I think is the least successful part of the book, was obviously not a timeline. Although clearly, as time has changed, investment advice has changed. But it was more or less a timeline. But what I did do before I started: I tried to think of as many interesting and humorous stories as I could, and I talked to people in the firm about it. I asked them, "Can you remember any great incidents in the history of the firm?" So those I wrote down as things that I had to include. Of course, because of the timeline they were spaced out so they do come in at intervals, which I think is quite nice.

As you were writing it, was there a little critic on your shoulder saying, "What will so-and-so think of this?" or "I shouldn't say this," or did you not worry at all? There are lots of references to people who weren't doing a very good job in their business.

Well, at that time, the amount of money the unit trust groups made was phenomenal. There was a huge bid and offer spread, and they were allowed to move it something like 13 per cent. So basically if there were more buyers than sellers of the funds, they could charge 13 per cent higher than they would give people back if they were selling when the fund was least popular. So they were making an absolute fortune. You could not get hold of a unit trust group manager on a Friday afternoon because they used to sit in a room and look at what was happening. They used to wait until Wall Street opened, and then they used to decide whether to create units or actually sell them because they could more or less guess what would happen, and they used to make a fortune on that.

When businesses make money very, very easily, there seems to be a propensity to allow people who are pretty useless to work for them. They don't clear out the dross. Some of the groups were very badly run. There was only one thing that mattered, only one thing. It was investment performance.

How did you come up with a title for your book?

Well, I thought of a better one afterwards! I didn't realise that there was a book called the same thing. It was all to do with the idea that, when I was at school, I worked out if I could persuade everyone in the country to give me a penny, I would make about £216,000 a year. This was old money, of course. I thought nobody would miss a penny. So I would try to work out how I could do that because £216,000 a year, when I was at school, was enormous. The Aishers, Sir Owen, and his brother David, used to take £100,000 a year, and they were the two highest paid men in the country. So £216,000 a year would have been very nice, thank you very much. Of course, that has been the whole thing: taking a small amount of money from a hell of a lot of people was a very good way to make a living. So basically, that was always the concept. We have now 700,000 clients, and we make a small amount of money out of each one.

There are a lot of other business books out there. Were you at all daunted by the idea of launching yet another business book?

Well, I thought mine was better than all the others. My book wasn't just ideas, it was common sense. There's one great book that I really love, it's called *Up the Organisation*, by a chap called Robert Townsend. There were some great ideas in that book. For example, I still love the one you should have on your wall in front of you: *Who do you want to least speak to today? Which task do you least want to do today?* Those are your top two priorities. Because otherwise, if you don't do them, they will be on your mind all day long.

You know, things like that are so important. There's something I need to do today, and I've been putting it off for weeks. I'm going on holiday on Friday, so I'm going to bloody do it or else I shall worry about it all the time I'm away.

That's the 'eat that frog' principle Brian Tracy talks about in his book, isn't it? Eat your 'frog' before breakfast. The same principle applies when you're resistant to just getting on and writing your book. What sort of feedback have you had from your readers?

Everybody that's read it has loved it. Literally. It's been so well received by people who read it. I've toyed with the idea of writing up the next seven years of it and sort of republishing it, taking out the investment bit. I think the business adventure idea is what is good about it, and the story of how we didn't obey any rules. For example, when we couldn't get a telephone in, we wrote 17 letters to British Telecom, on the basis that the squeaky wheel gets the oil. And the fight I had to get Bristol's best telephone number – sometimes you need to do things like that. All numbers in Bristol have to start with a nine, and the STD code is 0117. So, if your number begins with nine, what's the best number you could have? I thought it was 900-9000. So I managed to get that, and now we have that number which still is, without a shadow of a doubt, Bristol's best number.

Why do you not like the middle of your book, the investment bit? Why do you call it the least successful part?

You know, Mark Dampier has written a book about investment, and it's probably as good a stab as anyone has ever had. But it's not interesting. This is what you're up against in the investment industry. A lot of it is really very boring. But that's how you make money, by just hard work. There's nothing exciting. Only occasionally will you ever buy a share which travels because of a takeover bid a few weeks later. It's mostly persistence and hard work and confidence in what you're doing. And sticking to your guns.

Lots of fund managers go through bad periods, and the ones that succeed are the ones that don't worry about it. During the latter part of the millennium, around 1998 to 2000, it was the time of high-tech business, and Neil Woodford – who never bought a tech share the whole of that two years – had his worst time ever, because people were selling the shares he was in and were going for the risky, get-rich-tomorrow high-tech shares. He couldn't believe it. He thought, "Why are people buying these shares? They can't possibly be worth that!" These were companies that were valued at billions of pounds and didn't make a profit. How could that be? So he stuck to his guns, and of course, when the technology crash came about he was in all the stuff you should be in, and he became known as a genius.

My point is that most investment is very boring and nothing exciting, which makes for less interesting reading.

You name people you admire in your book. Also, people you perhaps don't admire so much! Did you feel vulnerable at times that you were perhaps exposing your opinions or speaking out too much?

I've always been terribly outspoken all my life. My father once said, "Your mouth will get you in trouble," but fortunately, it's never really got me in trouble. What people don't know is, I'm quite a sensitive chap in some ways. Sometimes I've done something or said something, which I've done on impulse, and I worry about it for days. Or even something from many years ago that I'm not happy with even now, and it sometimes comes back to my mind, and I think, "Well, I wish I hadn't done that." Sometimes I've pressed the send button on an email and thought, "Oh God. I wish I'd given myself five minutes, I wouldn't have sent that."

I think we're all guilty of that. So, let me have a picture of you when you were writing your book. What worked best for you: sitting at your desk at work, or did you prefer a more relaxed atmosphere at home?

I used to sometimes go in early to the office. I did it predominantly at home, though so I would take my little handheld chargeable Dictaphone home. You know, in those days it was a complete piece of machinery. I may have had two. Weekends were really when I did the most. I think the weather wasn't really great at the time, so that helped. It was done during the evenings at home too.

You're on the front cover of your book. How did you feel about having your photo on the cover?

I think it was right that I was on the cover because investment's an intangible thing. If we made aircraft, we could have put an aircraft on the cover. But we didn't – we provided investment advice. I had a young marketing director who said that we should be able to describe in six or seven words what we do. And of course, it's intangible. You can only show graphs and statistics, which is nothing to do with investment. So, in the end, I came up with: *help investors maximize their capital.* That's what we do in five words. We needed a way to convey that.

So how did you feel when you held your book for the very first time?

Proud. I was very proud. I did read the whole thing when it came out as a finished item, and I thought, "Peter, you haven't done a bad job there."

Were you nervous at all, about the book launch?

No, not really. I did sit on the settee on breakfast television with Kate Silverton and Bill Turnbull. That was brilliant. They were very good with me. Of course, this was after the business floated. You see, whilst I produced the book during that time, I don't think it got published until two years later.

I left it alone before we got going with it. It was quite strange really. By the time it was published, it was revealed that I was really quite wealthy.

Do you have any tips for other entrepreneurs who are hectically busy, and are wondering whether or not to write a book?

Well, if they're good at telling stories, and they're good at telling jokes, then there's a chance that they'll be able to do it. They don't have to be good at English or spelling, but they have to be a great storyteller. Otherwise, what they produce won't be of interest.

You mentioned perhaps rewriting your book. What are your plans now?

I am too quiet at the moment. I am finding it difficult to fill my life. I hate board meetings; they're absolutely no value whatsoever. So I resigned from all the boards of Hargreaves Lansdown about two years ago because I couldn't see the point in going. I was still working in the business at the time, although I'd appointed a new chief executive. In February 2015 whilst I was on holiday I had a very major heart attack, and sadly it left my heart very damaged and I had to have open heart surgery. My mitral valve got very damaged. In fact, during the heart attack, part of my heart wall died, so I don't have a muscle in one heart wall, and the muscles don't regenerate. So that meant that basically, I didn't go into the office for a long time, by which time the chief executive really felt that it was an opportunity for the firm to stand on its own two feet without me.

So I'm in that situation now. But I only have my family, and both my children don't live at home any more. I did go to the gym; I believed it was important that I was fit. I think you can't do a mental job if you're not fit, that's my view. But, suddenly I have all this time to spend. The other problem is when you run a business like Hargreaves Lansdown – which has been immensely successful, even if I do say so myself – anything you do is of very little consequence after that.

It feels like that success has never really been recognized. I'll put it in context. No one has ever created an FTSE100 company in their lifetime without borrowing acquisition. I mean, you can go out and take a company to the FTSE by acquiring businesses here, there, and everywhere, and you end up with very small amounts of the equity yourself, or borrowing vast amounts of money. Of course, we never borrowed a penny, and we never made an acquisition. So, it was completely organic growth. We started from my spare bedroom and created a FTSE100 company.

You might have heard of a little shop somewhere, and you occasionally might have gone in it. It's called Marks and Spencer. We're worth more than Marks and Spencer. Everyone thinks, "Marks and Spencer! All these wonderful people that run Marks and Spencer. Stuart Rose, Lord Rose." They pale in significance compared with what we did. We have computer systems to die for. We've invented, and we've written them all. How many pages do you think we have on the Hargreaves Lansdown website? About 180,000. And we hold about £70 billion of clients' money. And to think we've done all that and haven't borrowed a penny!

Summary for Super-Busy Entrepreneurs

- You don't need to be good at English or spelling to write a book. You do need to be good at telling jokes and a great storyteller.

- It may sound counter-intuitive, but it can help to write your book at your busiest time. This is because your brain is racing and you're feeling enthusiastic and excited.

- Use your business newsletters to jog your memory and help you come up with story ideas. This may also help you with a timeline to structure your book.

- Use a Dictaphone or voice recognition software to help you write your book, then get it edited.

- Write the book yourself rather than using a ghostwriter. No one will write the book like you, and your unique voice will come across.

- Be willing to have the final say with your editor. It is your book after all.

- Open your book with an attention-grabbing anecdote. Don't be afraid to be self-deprecating.

- Ask good friends or colleagues to remind you of interesting or funny anecdotes. Ask them what they remember most about you and also about the history of your business. Make a list of events to include in your book.

- Think of your original motivations and inspirations for setting up your business. This may well help you find your book title.

- Remember to check if anyone else has used your title already.

- Don't just have theory and ideas in your book. Give valuable life lessons and use common sense that your readers can use in their everyday lives.
- Think about times where you've broken the rules or had adventures in order to progress your business. Do these events provide valuable lessons for others?
- If you're writing about a "boring" topic, can you find a way to make it more engaging and interesting?
- Be bold and outspoken if a subject is close to your heart. Stand by your beliefs.
- Choose quieter times of day to write your book. Go early to your office. Or write it at home in the evenings or on weekends.
- Consider having your own photo on the front cover of your book, especially if you offer an intangible service.
- There's likely to be a delay between finishing your book and getting published if you opt for a traditional publisher.
- Re-read your manuscript after it's published and you have your paperback in your hands.

CHARLIE MULLINS, OBE

"People listen to you more if you've brought a book out… in a lot of people's eyes, you go up a level."

Charlie Mullins, OBE, is founder of London's largest independent plumbing company, Pimlico Plumbers.

It is the UK's first branded plumbing company with a clientele that includes: Simon Cowell, Dame Helen Mirren, Joanna Lumley, Joan Collins, Keira Knightly, Daniel Craig, and Richard Branson.

The business has a workforce of over 300 staff and £35 million turnover.

Charlie is a well-known TV personality who has starred on *Secret Millionaire*, *Show Me Your Money*, BBC's *Posh Plumbers*, and has regularly appeared on news programmes such as *Daily Politics* and *Panorama*.

He's author of *Bog-Standard Business: How I Took the Plunge and Became a Millionaire Plumber*, published in 2015.

People find what I've done, my working life, quite fascinating. So the real aim was to inspire others when I wrote my book. What I was trying to be was honest. I was saying: "If I can do it, you could do it." In other words, you don't really need a degree to be successful. That type of angle.

People had been nagging you for over a decade to write your book. Why did it take so long for you to get around to doing it?

I think I was frightened if I'm being honest. I was frightened to reveal things, maybe. It's all great if you say, "I've done this, and I've done that." But if you're saying, "I come from a poor background, and Mum and Dad were alcoholics. I had no money, and worked from the age of nine," that's different. So the reason I think I held back was, I didn't want people to know the truth.

While it was a bad upbringing, I don't think there was anything wrong with that. But we all like to let people think we've got loads of money. You don't normally reveal the bad side of things you've done, the struggles you've had in life. You tend to ignore them. I felt it just wasn't a story I wanted to tell until later on in life when things were getting better. All the good things came later in life: you get an OBE and appear on *Secret Millionaire*. What was holding me back was, I didn't want to reveal I'd had a tough life. I came from having no money to getting money, and I think you often want to hide that point.

So you felt quite vulnerable?

I think that's a better way of putting it, yes. A much better way.

When you were writing the book, were there things that you really struggled with, thinking, "Am I going to put this in or am I going to keep it out?"

Yes. I think I was trying to be fairly decent to my family. They've done nothing wrong, but when you start saying your mum and dad were alcoholics, and they spent more time in the pub, and they had no money even though they both worked. Those things you want to hold back, and second to that, you think, 'they're both dead now, and even if they were still alive, I don't want to be knocking or condemning family.' So that was quite worrying. People were saying, "You shouldn't be saying that about your parents." So I was probably being more protective if that makes sense? There were times we had no money and had no food, though I may not have over-expressed those points. I just didn't want to embarrass my family with anything I may say about them.

So you didn't want to be disrespectful to family or to their memories. This is something that most people feel when they're writing an autobiographical book or a memoir. Did you show your book to friends or family, to get feedback before it was published? Or did

you run it by a libel lawyer? Or was it just down to you, what you included?

I very much decided myself. I didn't dress it up. I kept it to the basics on certain things, and maybe I could have said a few more things. I felt comfortable with what I'd said in there. And yes, we did run it past lawyers to check there was nothing in there that was incorrect.

That might surprise some people, who think of you as being outspoken and saying what you think?

You are right there. But I think there are a couple of things I mention about Lord Sugar in there. You create a few enemies when you're successful in business. You upset a few people on your way. We wanted to make sure there would be no libel cases against me. But anything else that's in there, I didn't get anyone to approve of it. It came from my mouth, and I was fairly happy with what I was saying.

There are some very funny moments in your book. I laughed out loud when you told the men working for you, "It's haircuts, the lot of you," and said, "Anyone with a ponytail gets the sack." Did you decide to write your book or speak it?

I spoke it and recorded it. Some of the things we've done are different. Even today, some people are quite alarmed when we say, "No. Wrong hairstyle. Tattoos on your face. You're not presentable." A lot of what I wrote about happened 20 or 30 years ago, but people are still quite shocked by it now.

There's always a fear, I find, with entrepreneurs when they're writing books, that they're somehow giving away their business secrets if they write about their business too closely. What do you think about that? Did you worry about letting people know what really goes on in your business?

That didn't bother me in the slightest. Years ago when people were copying the business or copying the things we'd done, I'd get annoyed with it. I think in the end, you take it as a compliment when people say, "I love the uniform, love the number plates, love the tidy vans, love the tidy engineers." So I'm not bothered that somebody picks up business ideas.

What I've learnt is that it doesn't matter how many good ideas you have, it's still about the person behind it, the one running the show. If you have an orchestra, you could have 10 people with a trumpet and 10 with a guitar, and 10 with something else, but that orchestra is only any good if the conductor is. People copy Pimlico Plumbers all the time, but it doesn't make them Pimlico Plumbers. There's only one Harrods, there's only one Pimlico Plumbers. So it doesn't bother me. I think we've helped to improve the industry and upped the game. There was a bad stigma about the plumbing industry, and I think we've changed that. If you've gone up a level in business, it means you're busy. If we wore dirty clothes at work, the industry would go down. So I think we've improved the industry.

You've had a meteoric rise. You describe it as "going from street urchin to millionaire." These days you mix with movie stars and celebrities. David Cameron asked for your advice on how to sort out

unemployment among young people while he was Prime Minister. Why do you think you've been so successful?

The word is 'recognition'. I learned from my marketing department you could be the best company in the world, the best plumbers, but if nobody knows about you, then it doesn't matter. You need recognition, whatever it takes. And most of the time you want to be recognised for good things.

If you walk in a room, people need to know you're there. I always wear blue suits, and have done so for years because it's the colour of my company. I go to Downing Street, and they've got a black suit, blue suit, or pinstripe suit on. I go with a blue suit or something checked, and everybody, whether they like it or not, know you're there. You wouldn't believe the amount of people who come to me and say, "I recognise you by your hair." I speak to people I see in Downing Street and at the Conservative party conference, and I haven't got a clue who some of them are, but they seem to know me. Lord Digby Jones was speaking up in Mayfair, at a big gentlemen's club, and some guy came over to me – and it was packed out, everyone looked the same – and said, "Are you Charlie Mullins?" I said, "Yes," and he said, "I recognised you by your hair." I speak to people all the time, but there's nothing about them that makes me remember them.

So I quickly learned that it's all about recognition, and getting recognised for the right thing. Everywhere I go now, I get recognised. Even when I go abroad, people recognise me.

A lot of people might feel intimidated by the idea of mixing with stars and celebrities and that they might be patronised, or that they're not comfortable stepping up to that next level. Did you ever feel that, or did you just sense they were ordinary people the same as you?

I think in the very early stages, I felt I was out of my depth. I've been to Downing Street and thought, *'I'm not going to be able to deal with this.'* I went somewhere else and saw all these celebrities and felt, at first, intimidated and out of my depth. But now I just go to the party conference, in the meeting room, and I know most of them now. I'm the oddball out of them all, but I don't feel intimidated or embarrassed.

It was a bit like nobody would speak to you in the early days, but now people say, "Come and have a chat with us. Come and do this or that." I was at the Conservative party conference the other week, having a drink at the bar afterwards, and so many people were coming over. These are people from up north, and all over the country, everywhere. It was packed. One guy, he had a party of about 12, and he said, "Would you mind doing a very quick speech for us, and telling everyone who you are?" I thought, *'Are you sure?'*. It was the strangest place I've been asked to do a speech. But no, I don't feel intimidated. In the early days, yes, but now these people come over and talk.

Some of them say, "I'd like to have a conversation with you because you say it how it is." I think they get bored of their own type of people that don't speak the truth. In the beginning, I found it difficult to walk into a room full of people, and now, if someone asks me to speak in front of 500 people, it doesn't bother me in the slightest.

Do you have any tips for any other entrepreneurs or business owners who might aspire to step up to that level?

Something I say to myself sometimes – because some days I'm giving talks to business people – and I'm thinking, "Oh, this isn't going to work tonight, with the type of crowd they are, the type of business people they are." Sometimes I'm talking to budding entrepreneurs, and sometimes it's established business people, and I'm thinking, '*Surely you lot know more about business than me.*' I think I used to undermine myself thinking like that.

Now, I realise that I talk common sense. People can understand me. If someone asks me something, I make it as simple and direct as I can, so they understand what I'm saying. When I'm talking now, I realise that the types of questions they're asking are so basic. You think to yourself, '*If you're running a business, you should know that.*'

The amount of people who ask me, "What's the hardest thing about running a business?" Well, I've never found anything more difficult in business than employing people as your staff. Customers are simple, doing the job is simple, getting the money is simple. It's all about the people you employ. That's the hard thing about business. That's what I believe. Employing people and retaining them. Obviously, if you've got a good workforce, your business is better.

In your book you mention your conversation with David Cameron when he asked for your advice in sorting out youth unemployment. You were quite straightforward: you said to blow up all the Jobcentres and put school leavers into apprenticeships. Do you feel that a book can help to influence people and bring about change?

Undoubtedly it does. The people who get the most out of my book are youngsters trying to get into the workplace or an apprenticeship, or starting up their own business. I think the older ones are more likely to say, "I've been going 25 years, but I haven't really gone far. I started off with two people, and now I've got eight." They ask really stupid questions, like "I really want to expand, *but* ..." The only way you're going to expand in business is by employing people. It's the hardest thing, and people always try to avoid it. People tell me they want to make their business bigger, and they're already telling you, "I've got five people. At the moment, I'm doing the plumbing, and the estimating, and the wages. If I employ someone else, it's going to cost this much, or if I get another plumber ... I don't know what to do, but I'm going around in circles." And I say, "The answer's in the question. You're trying to do everything. You need to employ more people."

I think a lot of people do read the book and make changes. The amount of people, even established businesses that read the book and decide: '*I'm going to get my guys in uniform. I'm going to get a clocking-in machine; a canteen. I'm going to make sure we get work 24 hours.*' For me, they're all obvious things, and people say, "Well, they're obvious to you, Charlie, because you've always done them." A lot of these people haven't. I'm amazed at how many people every day, come up and say, "I've read about you – I've read the book, and I found it very inspirational." I didn't write it to say, "*Everyone should wear uniform and it'll be better for you*," but it's a bit of a no-brainer. A uniform's a must. Will it improve your business? Of course it will. People like you to turn up smart and tidy.

Does your book appeal mainly to readers in the UK, or to people in other countries too?

No, it's all over the world. I get people ringing me up who've seen me on a television programme. We get a lot of people from Australia and New Zealand, with plumbing companies or businesses, and they say, "When we come to London, is there any chance we can come and have a walk around and have a chat with you?" And you think, 'It's not a magic formula; I haven't got anything to sell.' I don't know whether it's lack of confidence. I think what a lot of people can't get their head around is: the simpler you keep it, the better. I think the reason why Pimlico Plumbers are so good is because the rest are so bad. We run the business on common sense. But common sense doesn't come with a degree, does it?

It's true. There are a lot of intelligent people lacking in it.

People complicate business, and we're not doing anything clever. We turn up on time, we do the job, and we collect the money. But they say, "Well, we don't start until ten, and we don't have uniform, and we have dirty old vans, and we go to the pub at night." They're just doing it wrong rather than doing it right. In the plumbing industry, most of them used to be scruffy and turn up late. We turn up early, and we're not scruffy.

You also have a large number of customised number plates on your vans.

We have about 150 plumbing-related number plates, and it was done for two reasons. One, as straightforward PR. They're very recognisable, even though I didn't think they would be 30 years ago, but that was what was in my mind. It was also a good investment. I bought the first number plate, and we now have about 150. The amount of people that recognise the company because of them! We have people asking for lists of them. We have kids doing the Eddie Stobart thing, looking out for them and spotting them. We have customers booking by the number plate.

So many people have copied it and are doing very well out of it. We do charity things with them like 'spot the number plate'. Sitting here thinking about it now, what an incredible PR idea! They've gone up in value. The biggest advertisement we have is our vehicles on the road. So the better they look, the more recognisable they are, the more we get recognised.

The title of your book, did you come up with it yourself? Or did you have a team of people working on it?

Our PR company worked on that one. There was a little team of people sitting around who came up with it. It wasn't my number one choice, so I can't really take the glory for that. They gave us various ideas, and we had our own ideas, and that was what they came up with.

I had a choice, but sometimes you're better off listening to other people. I'm a great believer that everyone is good at something, but you're not good at everything. Maybe I'm better at plumbing than book titles. I'm happy with that title now. It seems to fit the bill. People seem to smirk a bit when you say it.

Tell me what you did for the launch of the book. Did you have a launch plan and a marketing plan?

Oh, definitely, yes. We had a book launch at the Hippodrome Casino. We rented a theatre there, and it got filmed. I think it went out in America; someone sold the film off to a local airline. A chap called Neil Sean helped me. He's a presenter, and I met him and did an interview with him on a television show. Anyway, he asked, "So, how are you doing your book launch?" and we were going to do it at our company headquarters, with a few bottles of wine and invite some people. He said, "I don't think that's the best way to do it."

He actually did his own book launch at the London Palladium, I think. And I was thinking, '*I can't do the London Palladium. I'm a plumber!*' Anyway, he suggested the Hippodrome and told us what to do, and it was a great bit of advice. I think we had about 300 people there. It got a lot of attention and a bit in the press afterwards, and people still remember it now.

It's like anything. Some things have to be done properly. If it was left to me, I'd have done it at the depot, but this guy said, "I know what I'm talking about. Trust me." I would do it again, but at a bigger venue and make more of it.

So there's always a fear factor. No matter what you do, you've just got to push through it?

That's right. You've got to take risks. I know all these business entrepreneurs say that, but it's true. It probably cost us 10 grand to hold it there, so you're gambling, and you're thinking, '*Oh, what if people don't turn up?*' But it went down great. One of the things I've learnt in business is that we all undermine ourselves, and we don't think big enough. So now, I would go from the Hippodrome, not to London Palladium, but something in Shaftesbury Avenue, something in between.

There's always another level to move up to.

Yes. I think the main thing is that you must think big, but realistically. I've learnt that the more you think that, you grow into it. We bought the building we're in—I think it's about 30,000 sq ft—and we came from a 2,000 sq ft building, and at the time I was thinking, '*Am I doing the right thing? I've bought this great building, and we're plumbers?*'

Now we've run out of space. We own that building and another floor. So it was that sort of thinking ahead. I realise now that I could have bought a bigger building at the time. We're going to extend this building, and we're over the moon with it, but the average person doesn't think that far ahead. The bigger the jump, the higher the risk, but the bigger the reward.

What sort of impact would you say your book has had on your life and your business?

I'm going to answer that quick and direct. Tremendous. Incredible. It sort of puts you on the map. People listen to you more if you've brought a book out; I didn't realise that. In a lot of people's eyes, you go up a level. They say, "I didn't know you brought a book out." So you've gone from a normal person to maybe something special because you've got a book. A lot of people won't know the content, but if you can say you've brought a book out, people take more notice of you.

The amount of people that ask me about the book, or come up for advice, and I say, "Look, I'm not making any money out of my book. Anything we make we give to a charity, but the best advice I could give you is to buy my book." So I think, in writing a book, it takes you to a level where people take you very seriously. If you had said to me 10 years before it came out, "Are you going to write a book?" I'd have said, "Are you mad? Why would I write a book? What does a book give people?" For a few years, as we were getting nearer to it, I was turning it down because I was thinking no one would be interested. Now, I wish I'd done it 10 years earlier. Now, I want to bring another book out.

So you have plans for another book?

My mind has already told me I need to bring another book out. I don't think I need the autobiography side of it; I need the business side of it now. So many people are asking me the same questions: "How can I expand? What happens when you nearly go bust? What happens if you can't afford it? What happens when you can't buy a building? What happens if someone owes you money?" I'm getting asked so many questions, and most people might want to know a little bit about your personal story, and that's interesting. But what people really want to know is: what's the magic formula?

So it leverages your time, by answering the questions you're being asked over and over again?

Exactly. I'd give anyone advice, but I just don't have the time, and it becomes expensive. We get so many people ringing us up, or emailing saying, "I'm in London; could I pop in for half an hour? Could I ... could I ... could I ...?" I did it for a little while, and I haven't got a problem with it. You can ask me a question, and I'll give you my answer to it.

So now we do tours here: Pimlico Tours. There's got to be a minimum of 10 people who put £150 in, and we give them a book, lunch, a toy car. We have two hours of walking around the building, talking. Then we have lunch, and they get all the information they want. We give the £150 to charity – I'm not doing it for the money. It just stops all the people who want to spend an hour with you and buy you a coffee.

The tours go down quite well. We've had people come from Holland, we've had people come from France. And I'm thinking, '*Are you sure?*

You're getting a plane to come on one of our tours?' I find it funny. But I think our building is very inspirational. We've got it all geared up properly and different departments. I'm looking out of my office now, and the accounts is outside of me, and all the people are at their desks, and they're getting on with their work. It's very regimental and organised, and I think people are quite taken aback by that. We do tours for schools and colleges and The Prince's Trust – obviously we don't charge them – and them walking around the workplace for two hours and having lunch, it totally inspires people and changes their views on the workplace.

Tell me about the charity and how that works with your book.

There's a local girl in Pimlico, Chloe. She's got cancer, a very rare one, and she's getting treatment. I think she's about four years old now, she might be five. Being a local girl, we were asked if we could help out. So we did, and we raised loads of money. We put a picture of her on our vans, saying "please donate" and various charity things. Then I came up with the idea that 10 per cent of the book proceeds would go to her charity. So every so often, we check how many have been sold and send her a cheque. The book wasn't done to make money. The book was done because people keep asking the same questions. I don't mean that being miserable. If you do a little charity with it, it works in a few ways. One, you're helping someone, the second thing is that it makes you feel good, and the third thing is, it's great PR.

The little girl is just a personal thing. But when we're involved with The Prince's Trust or The Barry Daniels' Trust, that's a bigger scale. I've just come back from Spain and was involved with a pink ball out there; it's a charity I've been involved with for a number of years. I mean, everyone knows somebody who has got cancer or died with it. I think there's a feel-good factor, it makes people in the company feel good that you're not all about being a greedy plumber. And, what goes around comes around. You do get a lot of return back from it.

Your book is available for Kindle and hardcover only. Why no paperback?

I've got no idea. I have no idea if a hardcover sells more than a paperback. I left that to the publisher, John Blake. I never gave it a thought. I had one meeting with him, and we went in the room, which was his office—a massive office in Fulham—and all the walls were lined with books. He said, "These are all the people I've done books for," and it was people like Princess Di, Katie Price; all the footballers; top singers; celebrities. The place was packed with them. So I just left it to him – he obviously knows more about it than me. My own view is that I don't think paperbacks look as credible as a proper hardcover book. But I left it to him.

Something else you might be interested in. I met an Indian guy called Rami Ranger. He came up here and was doing something for television. He distributes products for supermarkets all over the world. Massive businessman, and his book's called, *From Nothing to Everything*. Another bit on the front says, *From £2 to £200 Million*. A funny thing about books is, if you brought a book out and someone else has too, the deal is that you exchange books. So he came up to me and said, "Look, I'd like to exchange books with you. I'd like one of yours, and I'm giving you mine." And I thought, *'I've never heard of that before.'* So he signed a special message, and I did the same.

He's a good guy who came from nothing. It was looking at his book that made me want to bring another book out, and I think it'll be better than the first one. I like how they lay it out in his book. Immediately I opened his cover, he had the right pictures: the Queen, Margaret Thatcher and a few other Prime Ministers, and I thought, *'That's clever'*. Every time you flicked, there was this little bookmark, but it was part of the book. I thought, *'How clever is that?'* He's got the message straight across. I haven't read it yet, but I've started to. He's told me his story, and it's got to be an incredible story. I like this idea that you exchange books, and it was something I'd never heard about. He tells people, "I've met Charlie, and we've exchanged books." How nice is that? I don't often mention that I've written a book. I only bring it up when people want advice or if they say, "Have you ever thought about bringing a book out?" So I tell them, and they say, "You're joking. Blimey." I think it's a big thing to bring a book out; I just wish I'd done it earlier.

Summary For Super-Busy Entrepreneurs

- Aim to inspire others with your story. The underlying message is: "If I can do it, you can do it."
- You may initially have a fear factor that stops you writing your book. You may feel vulnerable about revealing the struggles you've had in life or embarrassing your family.
- Have your book checked by a libel lawyer if you're outspoken and think your book might offend others.
- Don't worry about revealing too many of your business secrets or people stealing your ideas. They can mimic you, but they never will be you.
- Recognition is vital. You can be the best at what you do, but if no one knows about you, it doesn't matter.
- Wear clothes or a hairstyle that make people notice and remember you. Wear your business branding colours if possible.
- At first, you may feel out of your depth or afraid to walk into a room full of people when stepping up to the next level. But over time, it will become easier.
- Avoid undermining yourself with negative talk or believing that others know more than you. Often, they are just looking for simple common sense.
- Don't assume that because something is obvious to you, it will be so to everyone else.
- Don't be afraid to speak your mind even if what you say is controversial. Books can be powerful influencers in bringing about change, upping the game, and raising industry standards.

- Customised number plates are powerful PR as they're memorable and recognisable. They're also a good investment.
- You may not be the best person to think of your book title. Ask you PR team to work on ideas and suggestions.
- Think big with your book launch. There may be a worry that people won't turn up, but try to push through it.
- Consider hiring a theatre or other venue for your book launch, rather than using your business premises.
- A book puts you on the map. Even if people haven't read your book, they take you more seriously.
- When people ask you the same questions again and again or want to "spend an hour with you and buy you coffee", leverage your time by suggesting they read your book.
- Consider combining your book with a tour of your business that includes lunch, a talk, and a gift.
- Consider giving a percentage of your book proceeds to charity. It helps others, makes you feel great, and it's good PR.
- Hardback books have more kudos than paperbacks.
- Exchange books with other authors, and write a special message in the front to leave a lasting impression.

MALCOLM WALKER CBE

"It was cathartic for me to write ... I wanted to set the record straight."

Sir Malcolm Walker CBE was co-founder of a small frozen food shop called Iceland in 1970, setting it up as a sideline while working as a trainee manager in Woolworth's. He built up the business from nothing to a company with annual sales of over £5 billion, employing 30,000 people and giving £10 million to charity.

He left Iceland under a cloud early in 2001 when the company was taken over, but returned four years later to transform its performance. Today, Iceland is recognised as one of the Best Companies to Work for in the UK. Malcolm is author of *Best Served Cold: The Rise, Fall and Rise Again of Malcolm Walker*, published in 2013.

I was writing the book for me, really. Don't forget, I'd just been fired under traumatic circumstances. The book was published in 2013, but 90 per cent of it was written back in 2001. We waited to find a publisher, and then the last bit was added on to the end in 2013.

I'd just been fired. I was planning to retire anyway, but actually, getting pushed, the circumstances were quite traumatic. Instead of being remembered as the guy who'd built a big business, created thousands of jobs, done all good things, I was suspected of being a crook because I'd sold shares before a profit warning. The wheels grind very slowly, and it took three-and-a-half years before I was cleared. If you read the section of the book about my successor Bill Grimsey, you'll understand the issues, because any new chief executive coming into a company will obviously clear the decks. But there's clearing the decks and then there's clearing the decks. He was very good at his own PR, and he portrayed it as: he took a job with a company where he thought it was going to be a well-run business and a touch on the tiller was all that was required, but when he came in, it was a complete bag of shit.

So, leaving the business under those circumstances, let's say it was a bit cathartic for me to write the book. I wanted to also set the record straight, which is impossible to do in a press interview because it's edited down to a few paragraphs, and there will be a few sides of the story. I actually wanted to get my story across, so I wrote the whole book in maybe six months, and then sort of forgot about it. I got back into Iceland, and it was quite a few years later when I thought, 'I'd better finish this book.' Whilst it took me maybe nine months to write the first eighty per cent, the final 20 per cent I just knocked off in three days.

So you didn't know, when you first wrote it—when you wanted to put the record straight—what the ending was going to be? You had another ending in mind?

That's right. It's the chronological recording of events. You know, I really enjoyed writing it. There was a lot of personal research from the memory bank, from memorabilia at home to get dates and different things. It was an interesting thing to do, and then you think, 'Hmm, it'll be great for the children one day.'

You say that you forgot about it. Was that just because life took over? Obviously, you went back to Iceland.

Getting around to it was quite difficult and, also, I didn't really know where the ending was going to be. And I had tried every now and again to find a publisher, without much success. Because I hadn't finished it.

Did you find it a difficult or easy process writing your book?

I wrote it, and then I thought I'd get someone to rewrite it in proper English. I did have someone make a start on that and then decided my version was better than his. So every word in the book was actually written by me.

And you blend elements of your personal life and your business life in the story...

It's a business autobiography, and I brought in personal events only when I thought it was necessary to mark the time or put things into context. I didn't want to get too much into personal things, but there is a little bit of my personal life in there. But not too much.

Your wife plays quite an important part, doesn't she? She's mentioned quite frequently because she's been a pivotal person supporting you throughout your business life.

Yes, of course. She was supportive from the day we started: she was the breadwinner. Yes, she was very supportive. Also, when it all went wrong, she was as upset as I was.

So how did you decide—because obviously there's lots of things going on in your life—what to keep in, what to take out?

I put in everything I could think of, business-wise. I put all the adventures in, tried to do it year by year, as things went along, and then just interjected things which I thought were important milestones in my personal life, like getting married or buying a house or having children.

So the milestones, the important events. And you start your book with what must have been one of your most difficult points of your life.

You have to have a grab-attention opening, don't you?

I totally agree, but I have to say not every author realises that. You'd be surprised how many books take a while to warm up, and then come up with a dramatic event around page 30.

It would have been quite boring if I had started at the beginning, you know? I thought, 'Well let's have the drama first and then go back.'

Did you feel vulnerable sharing the inner workings of your mind? Did it bother you to think that your competitors – maybe even your enemies – might be reading all this?

No. Not at all. It was all business. There's very little personal in there. I describe it as a business autobiography.

You've sometimes had to deal with hostile journalists and negative treatment from the press. Have you got any tips for entrepreneurs who might be nervous about handling press interviews?

Yes, ignore it, and don't take them too seriously. If there's a bad one, I get a bit bloody wound up about it, but sometimes you've got to temper your views. I suppose as a public company, that's when it's most difficult because you're having to pander to the teenage scribblers. At the half-year results, we'd do an analyst's presentations, and then we'd have to go and visit the 10 biggest shareholders. That would usually be the top floor in a lavishly furnished boardroom with about 10 people, under 25, sitting around the table asking inane questions. And when we left, just as they were discussing what we do with Iceland shares – do we hold them, sell them, buy more, whatever? – we'd be saying, "Would you trust your life-savings to dickheads like that?"

So do you do any preparation before interviews with journalists?

You know the phrase 'winging it' is best. I've never considered we're a proper company. Process, procedure, corporate governance, steering groups, committees, that was Bill Grimsey. And that is most companies, really. I'm quite happy when people describe me as a cowboy or maverick. It's about getting things done. Which is why the world is horrified that Donald Trump's been voted in. I think he might be quite good, actually. I do. Really. Seriously. Because America's voted for change. And they certainly wouldn't get it with Hillary, and the fact he's had zero experience as a politician is probably bloody good. It's that fresh pair of eyes. Don't get sucked into bureaucracy.

You've been on a BBC documentary about Iceland. What did you learn from the experience, and would you do it again if you were asked?

I learned not to do it again. We'd been asked many, many times to do that kind of thing and always turned it down because you're not in control. Somehow, I got convinced by the filmmaker that they were going to do a fair job. Thinking about it, I thought this could be good PR for Iceland—because at that point we needed it. So it was a risk. So we had a go. There was maybe six months of filming which was edited down into three one-hours. The producer filmmaker guy had never been in an Iceland, but pretty soon he became a disciple and a great admirer of the company. He was very much on our side. But all that footage was probably given to some *Guardian*-reading girl in London –who'd got preconceived ideas about Iceland – and edited in an appalling way, so that when we were shown the preview, even without any editorial control, I said, "If you show that, I'll sue you." It was doctored to make us look even more downmarket than we already were. It was horrendous. Then I instantly regretted giving them free access, as we had, rather than just being on top of what they were filming. They did alter it. Not a lot, but a bit. The end result of that was that I've not met anybody—well, one person—who hasn't said what a brilliant thing it was. I said, "What! As a comedy show?" And they said, "Your company came over great, and as a great place to work." It's true it did, in that our job websites exploded. It put the company's culture in a good light, but it did put us as a really downmarket business, and that is the one reason I wouldn't do it again. Unless I got complete control on the editing.

So you're not really an advocate of "any publicity is good publicity". It's more about maintaining the correct branding?

I suppose really, you see, I'm contradicting myself. Lots of people thought it was very good. But I know it just reinforced our downmarket credentials.

Your book came out around the same time. What did you do for your launch? Was it low-key or a big event?

Our PR hasn't been very good: we've never achieved much positive press. More recently we have, and it's about a few new people we've got working in the business. I really do think in the last three months, in particular, we're making quite a bit of headway. But coming back to the book launch, it basically went off like a damp squib. We had a drinks do at a restaurant in London, and that was about it, really.

A lot of the interviews in the press mention your book.

Purely by coincidence – the BBC were convinced it was a Machiavellian plot – purely by coincidence, the book was published a week after the last episode of the TV series was aired. So there were a lot of interviews around that time that were either inspired by the BBC wanting publicity for the series or by the publisher wanting to plug the book.

So that worked in your favour?

I've forgotten what the actual end results were as opposed to those we gave away or were sold half-price through the shops. But for a week, it was the bestselling business autobiography, just for one week. If you've been on Amazon and read the reviews, they're all five-star. I don't know how many we sold in the end, I've lost track. I couldn't make a living out of it, that's for sure.

Do you keep copies of your book in your briefcase or use it as a kind of business card?

We gave a paperback copy to every one of our 850 store managers, and we put the paperbacks on sale in the stores. We sold a few, I don't know how many. But the hardback, through Amazon, we've sold low thousands, I think.

I'd have thought, if you were on the speaking circuit, you'd have a lot of interest from entrepreneurs and small business owners.

It's done, I've had it published, that's it. I'd rather sell fish fingers now.

The proceeds from your books are going to Alzheimer's charities. Tell me a little more about that and the impact that has?

Well, linked in with us being the best company in Britain to work for, two years out of three, we do a lot for staff morale. It's a big thing in Iceland; the culture of this business is like no other. One thing we do is our charity week in August, where the stores can do whatever they want to raise money for charity. Over the last few years, we've given around £10 million to charity, and we always choose a smaller charity where we can make an impact. No throwing a pebble in The Pacific you know. So we've given various charities our million pounds, and the last few years we've given it to Alzheimer's research because Alzheimer's kills more people in Britain now than any other illness. That was on the radio this morning.

One in three people alive today will die of it, but nobody knows what causes it, and there's no cure. Because it's an unfashionable thing, nobody likes to talk about it: Cancer Research Campaign raises over £100 million a year; Alzheimer's research raises £6 million. So, we've given £3 million over three years, but now we're doing more than that. You know the carrier bag levy, the five pence you pay for the carrier bag? We're giving £10 million over three years to the University College of London towards a new dementia research centre, but we're also getting other retailers to join in, and we reckon we'll raise £25 million, which will be enough to trigger-fund the £350 million that they're going to spend on this, so I believe that we'll make that happen. It wouldn't have happened otherwise because they were short of funding, so the reason why we do this in store every year is partly because it's the right thing to do, and partly because the staff enjoy it: it's fun, it's bonding, and the staff love to get behind events like that.

There's a lot of middle-class snobbery around shopping at Iceland, when do you think you should listen and not listen to what people say?

We started in 1970, and every year, barring a tiny blip, we increased our profits to the year 2000. So, for 30 years, we increased our sales and profits. There aren't many, if any, other companies in Britain that have done that. It all went wrong the four years I was away; the company lost money. Then, when I came back in 2005, over the next few years, profits grew every year until about three years ago when they peaked at about £230 million. So I know who our customer is: it's Kerry Katona. I didn't care what people thought about our customer base because it was a money machine. The last two or three years the world has changed, and without going into great detail (it's not just Aldi and Lidl – there's a hundred things that have changed) we've had to reassess where we are and broaden our appeal.

Our PR has improved massively in the last few months because of what we're doing in the business. But it's not an easy thing to do, to shift people's perception. I'll admit there's a stigma associated with shopping in Iceland: a third of the population of Britain wouldn't be seen dead in an Iceland. The Waitrose shoppers. Well, I didn't care. *Now* I do, and we're trying to address that. It's starting to have some success, not just in terms of PR, but in terms of sales growth. I believe we've turned the corner not just in terms of sales growth but in profit growth. I could talk all day on this, but I won't. The number of times I've sat at a dinner party and the woman sitting next to me will ask: "What do you do?" and she'll say, "I don't eat frozen food." Well, of course you do. Most things you eat have been frozen, but of course, you don't know that.

Take sea bass for instance. It's actually farmed in Greece. If it's sold as fresh, but it's about 10 days old when you buy it. Even sardines from Cornwall, they can't get to your fishmonger in less than five or six days. There is no such thing as genuinely fresh fish. It's usually 10 or 12 days old. So you're buying defrosted fish. So, for example, red snapper comes from Malaysia – frozen – it takes 45 days to get here. Ours goes into the shops still frozen. At most other supermarkets it's defrosted and sold as if it's fresh.

You've said in the past, "never be afraid of being called mad". Tell me how that philosophy has helped you throughout your life.

It's about doing unconventional things, because most sensible people are that: *too sensible*. I mean, to throw up a job and start a business, sensible people don't do that. It's just your attitude to life, really, and about being prepared to take a risk and do the unconventional. I mean, that's probably led to some of our greatest successes in terms of sales. If you think about this concept: you come into one of our stores, you pay for your shopping, you leave it, and we'll deliver it home to you, free of charge, within a ten-mile radius (and I'm not talking about online shopping here).

Well, that's mad. How can you possibly make money out of that? But we do. When we launched it, in 1996, the city thought we were off our head. But, thinking of that idea, you dismiss it immediately because it's mad. But you've got to try things.

You sometimes say you didn't do very well at school. You left with four O-levels from four attempts. Why do you think you've been so successful?

Perseverance. I had a great home life, but my dad died when I was 11. My dad worked down the pit. My family background wasn't academic, so I wasn't pushed at home. Whether I was lazy or rebellious or whatever, I wasn't really interested in school. Now, obviously, I've got a different attitude toward my own children: get your degree first and then see where you go from there. I thought I was going to be a carpenter, and then I joined Woolies.

And then you took a very different path. Iceland's been voted the best big company to work for. Why do you think you're better at this than your rivals?

We're unconventional. We have a conference; the conference itself is less important. It's the get-together, the fireworks, the party at night. It's a morale thing. Every year, it gets bigger and bigger, culminating in us chartering three jumbo jets and flying 1000 managers for a weekend at Disneyworld in Florida. It costs over £4 million. I mean, what public company can do that? You can't. But every penny of that is an investment in morale. When we have events, we have a free bar, for example. We don't close it. Alcohol's a good lubricator, really.

Which goes back to your phrase of never being afraid of being called mad. I take it from your comment about wanting to sell fish fingers that you don't want to write another book?

No, I really did enjoy writing that, and I do enjoy writing when I get around to it. I have a column every few weeks in *Retail Week*. If I've got time, and I can get started, I enjoy it.

Summary for Super-Busy Entrepreneurs

- A book allows you to tell your side of the story that has yet to be heard or understood.
- A book can highlight all the good things you've achieved, and ensure that this is what you're remembered for – for example, if you've been receiving negative media coverage.
- A book allows you more space to go into greater detail whereas press interviews are usually very brief and condensed.
- Writing a book can be cathartic, especially after traumatic events.
- You may not know the ending to a book when you write it. But the ending will eventually come to you.
- A book is a great legacy to leave for your children one day.
- A ghostwriter or editor may not write your book as well as you do. If you have two versions to compare, you may find that yours is better.
- With a business autobiography, bring in personal events to mark the time or put things in context. Interject important milestones in your personal life such as getting married, buying a house or having children.
- Choose an attention-grabbing opening for your book to hook in your readers.
- Write about dramatic events first before reverting back to less dramatic detail – even if this doesn't follow the natural chronology of events.
- Try to ignore press criticism, and don't take it too seriously.
- Not all publicity is good publicity. Think carefully before agreeing to take part in any TV documentaries.

- With media appearances, bear in mind that you may not be in control and that days and days of filming may be edited down to hours or minutes.
- PR can be risky. You may be shown a preview of TV footage, but you will have limited editorial control.
- Think long and hard whether you should give a journalist free access to your business or whether to be on top of the filming.
- Put books on sale in your business outlets, and put them on offer at half-price.
- Give your books away to your staff if you have a business as a "thank you" and a token of your appreciation.
- Consider giving away proceeds from your book to a charity of your choice.
- Do unconventional things and take risks that other "sensible" people won't.
- Don't dismiss an idea because it seems mad. "Mad" ideas can sometimes be your most lucrative.
- Perseverance can be more powerful than academic performance when it comes to success. Don't let lack of qualifications put you off.

DAN S. KENNEDY

"If I want to add another racehorse to my stable or acquire another classic car, I can write it."

Dan S. Kennedy is a multi-millionaire serial entrepreneur. He is marketing advisor, consultant, and coach, influencing over one million independent business owners annually through his newsletters, tele-coaching programs, and study groups.

As a speaker, Dan has appeared with four former U.S. Presidents, with Hollywood celebrities, and with business celebrities like Donald Trump, Zig Ziglar, Jim Rohn and Tony Robbins. For more than 10 consecutive years, he averaged speaking to more than 250,000 people per year, sometimes addressing audiences as large as 35,000.

He is author of the popular *No B.S.* books series.

First, let me say that I appreciate being identified as a 'celebrity' author. Not everyone would agree! Actually, I am, by deliberate design, a famous person nobody's ever heard of – and I'll come back to that when we talk about book promotion. But, to your question, I've written a total of 34 books that have been published, a few more that have not – 27 are currently in print. One just out of print, retired by its publisher, that I'm sorry to see go is a unique book: *The New Psycho-Cybernetics,* co-authored with the late Dr. Maxwell Maltz. The *No B.S.* book series at Entrepreneur Media (the publisher of *Entrepreneur Magazine),* is the longest running series, with the first book in it published in 2004, although it's a revision of an edition first published by a different publisher in 1993. The most recent in this series is the updated second edition of the *No B.S. Guide to Marketing to the Affluent,* released early in 2015. There are 14 books in this series. All my books are non-fiction; on entrepreneurship, business, advertising, marketing, and wealth subjects, with the exception of the aforementioned, broader self-help book with Dr. Maltz and two mystery novels co-authored with Les Roberts. Amazon has nearly all of them available.

What inspired you to write your very first book?

'Inspired' is *not* the best description of why I started having books published. For me, it was and is, more *pragmatic* than inspired.

All the major figures of the golden age of advertising in the U.S. in the 1950s had what I now call a "positioning book". This includes Ogilvy, Burnett, Hopkins, and others. Their books positioned them as thought leaders and as important people in the field and described their philosophy of advertising. At the beginning, I was narrow-focused in advertising, as a sales letter specialist, so I first self-published a positioning book titled *How To Write A Million Dollar Sales Letter* in 1979, which was re-done and trade-published by a small house, Adams Media, in 1981 as *The Ultimate Sales Letter*, followed in 1983 by *The Ultimate Marketing Plan*. These books have stayed in print, through four editions each, never off bookstore shelves to the present: 35 and 33 years respectively. They served as positioning books, in essence, replacements for calling cards and professional brochures, as principal tools in securing writing, consulting, and even speaking engagements, and directly as a marketing channel. Over the years, literally tens of millions of dollars of revenue has originated with one of these books being discovered and purchased by somebody off a bookstore shelf, in FedEx stores, lately on Amazon, then that reader coming into my membership organization, subscribing to newsletters, attending events or retaining me privately. The royalties from the books, incidentally, are insignificant by comparison to these revenues originated by the books.

All the major figures in the 'success movement' or success industry where I've also lived and worked for over 40 years also had positioning books. You can go back to the 1920s and 30s. Prime example: Napoleon Hill's *Think And Grow Rich*, 1937. In the success motivation field's golden age, post World War II 1950s to 1970s: Dale Carnegie; Norman Vincent Peale; Zig Ziglar, a 10-year speaking colleague of mine. And so on.

It just seemed obvious to me that you *needed* such a book in order to establish yourself as an important and authoritative figure in a field. Beyond that, I believe the axiom: publish or perish.

Beginning in 1999, I've averaged two new or revised edition books every year, with four different trade publishers – from giants like Penguin and

Prentice-Hall to the small houses like Adams Media and Entrepreneur, *and* with pay-to-publish houses like Advantage, and self-published by entities I own or have interest in. Many of these books are *micro*-positioning books. When I decided to add a newsletter to the stable on marketing to especially affluent clientele and saw the related trends as important to my audience, I wrote the book in the *No B.S.* series on that subject. When the boom of boomers as highest value consumers presented itself, I wrote the *No B.S. Guide to Marketing to Leading-Edge Boomers and Seniors*. When I decided to focus on financial advice and health care professionals, I wrote the *No B.S. Guide to Trust-Based Marketing*.

There's no spontaneous inspirational combustion involved in any of this. It has all been, in total, and each has been a calculated choice for specific business purposes.

I think, by the way, that most writers are delusional and naive about being a published author and what it alone can and can't do for you, so they often start with their grand, inspired idea of what *they* want to write about. That's why and how P.L. Travers wrote *Mary Poppins* – and if Walt Disney hadn't saved her, she'd have spent her late years as a pauper. The chances of being a J.K. Rowling in fiction or a Steven Covey in business books is far, far worse than the chances of winning the lotto *and* being struck by lightning *and* having whatever actor or actress you've fantasized about having sex with arrive at your doorstep naked and in lust – all at the same moment in time. I've worked backwards from business purposes and plans to do books, and each book has had attached to it and behind it an eco-system of its own to generate money and has been integrated into a bigger eco-system of income streams.

Why keep writing books? What motivates you?

The 'why', a plural answer, is there less and less, with age, accumulated body of work, absence of any financial need or need for exposure or client attraction, changes in my business life – the sale of my main membership business (GKIC.com) as example, and the changes in the publishing world as well … so I see my run at this soon ending. The question of why I should *keep on writing* new books rears its head with increasing frequency. While I am motivated by having something to say, and by an existent audience in waiting for whatever book I choose to do next, my chief reasons for writing books or for any other work is: money. And writing my books pays much less than writing marketing and sales materials for my clients, home study course type information products priced upwards from $1,000, and the monthly newsletters and other content I write for GKIC.

It was Mark Twain who said, "Anybody who writes but for money is a blockhead." It's why I've never kept a diary. So, I've continued writing books and getting them published, promoted, and distributed because being on bookstore shelves has been a very important and, more indirectly than directly, a financially rewarding place for me to be. Early, it was a necessary place. In more recent years, no longer necessary, but still the best means of being discovered by the best customers for GKIC and the best clients for me.

For quite a few years, there has been an 'income at will' factor to my writing – of books, but also of more elaborate and much higher priced information products, and of seminars. John Lennon said, "If we want one, I just sit down and *write us* a swimming pool." Similarly, if I want to add another racehorse to my stable or acquire another classic car, *I can write it.* So that, frankly, prompts a decision to do another book now and then. I own over 20 racehorses, so I do work – and write – for oats and veterinarians' kids' college tuition.

Although I haven't owned GKIC for many years, I have been a contract player, and my responsibilities encompass rain-making; supporting both new member acquisition and member retention, and a new book aids with both. To the latter, being the author of the next new book serves to *reinforce the positioning* of thought leader and important person, reinforcing people's desire for association. My chief publisher continues asking for a next new book. So there are a number of answers to your 'why' question.

Share with me your writing routine. Do you prefer music in the background or silence? Pen and paper, or a laptop?

My process is, first and foremost, gestational. I *never* face a blank page. So, over months, raw material is gathered randomly on a subject – from my own accumulated work like years of past newsletters, from research done for me, from open sources like others' books, magazine articles, online resources, experts I have relationships with, and so forth. Then it is organized into piles with titles. Ultimately, each pile is for a chapter. Finally, the stuff in a pile gets shuffled into a sensible order. From that, I load content into the computer, as is, or rewritten or written around as I go. When the loading is completed, I go back and convert the mess into finished content. I'm a two to, at maximum, three-draft writer. Locked in a room, starting with those piles in organized condition, I can do one of my business books in the equivalent of about 40 hours. No book is permitted much more because I have a pre-set, minimum hourly income required for my time, and I know what the book is likely to produce in direct income from royalties, co-author fees, and promotional fees, so that total divided by the hourly rate dictates the number of hours a book can be given. Most writers just write until they're done, and many never get done. Or they're working for minimum wage without even thinking about it.

As to the creative process, I work mostly in a cloistered and controlled success environment absent of distraction or interruption. I don't personally use the Internet, ever, for anything, so my computer is a typewriter and file cabinet. Not connected. No email to check or send, no social media to check, no games to play. I write at a desk in a room with no windows, with all my reference resources accessible, and a lot of space, because I am a "piler" not a "filer." I print work out on paper and mark it up by hand, write on the backs of pages by hand. But mostly I type, and my mind is trained to work the minute my fingers touch the keyboard. I began typing at about age eight, and the keyboard and conscious and subconscious minds have long ago melded. I also assign work to my subconscious overnight or during naps, and wake with writing done, to be quickly loaded. Mostly, I write in silence, but I will occasionally have music on, or the TV on – football games during season, for example.

I write to benchmarks, deadlines, and the clock. As I said, a book or any other writing has a pre-determined maximum amount of time it can be allowed based on its monetary value. This divides into benchmarks like number of pages that must be done per hour. My days are time scripted, so writing a newsletter may start at 7:00 a.m. and *have to be* done at 11:30 a.m. My subconscious has become well conditioned in performing under these requirements. I tend to automatically hit the right word count for a

12-page newsletter, for example, without ever counting words or pages. I hand the raw copy over, and it formats perfectly. You told me this chapter for your book needed to come in between 3,500 and 5,000 words, and I'll wager that I landed there with these answers' total – without ever doing any word counting or editing based on a word count. Nor, in this case, was there an outline.

How do you plan your books – and decide on the title and subject matter?

Subject matter is decided on by various means. I may identify the next micro-category within a genre, say, in marketing, like one of the examples I described above. I may have a co-author available or come forward, who will pay a significant fee for the privilege and has legitimate expertise and experience with the particular subject, a significant promotional platform of his or her own, and complementary views. Many of the most recent books in the *No B.S.* series were decided on because of the availability of a co-author. On a couple occasions, publishers have requested books on a subject of their choosing. My own core audience that puts a certain, solid floor under sales is well understood; I know them well, and I know what *won't* interest them. I also have a defined persona and can't wander off into the weeds and do something inconsistent. Some ideas *I* might be interested in writing about get discarded because of these governing factors.

It is *almost never* whim or merely something that interests me. In 40 years, I've indulged myself on only four occasions. For example, I wrote and had published a book titled *Make 'Em Laugh And Take Their Money*, about the use of humour as a platform sales speaker, and sales or advertising copywriter. I am a *very* serious student of the subject, it interests me; I'm a skilled practitioner, and I've worked intimately with people like the late Joan Rivers, a joke writer for Bob Hope and Johnny Carson. I wanted to codify my experience in a book. I knew it would have a very limited audience and serve none of my usual business purposes, but I did it anyway literally as an indulgence. My mystery novels with Les Roberts are an indulgence; the money is miniscule to me, and they serve no business purposes. Some would call this a 'bucket list item', and I *am* 60 years old, thus on the back nine with clubhouse in sight. But these are extremely rare, odd exceptions to my rules.

The business books are *planned* by purpose, by marketing and promotion that can be done or obtained for them, by audience, and by extraction of money from them. Stories about people or companies or case histories that demonstrate the teaching are, for example, chosen, first, based on who might pay me a promotional fee to be integrated into the book in that manner and be likely to buy quantities of books and/or have ability to promote the book, or, second, absent the payment of a fee, at least likely to buy quantities of books and/or have ability to promote the book. I do this much the same way that movie producers handle product placement in movies: a car chase not essential to the plot, created because there is a car company willing to pay to showcase their cars in it, and the chase goes through a Burger King parking lot because Burger King is willing to pay. On par, I match to as much as triple my royalty income from a book with such placement and promotional fees and I also establish a lot of promotional support for the book in advance. That negates need to dip into my pocket for advertising – although I have, at times, used the promotional fees to fund advertising, including full-page ads in over 30 different national magazines. In short, book planning is, for me, all about two things: Income. Promotion.

Do you find it hard coming up with fresh ideas?

No. The opposite. I have more than 20 active files on my computer at this moment, each for a possible book. Time permitting and satisfactory compensation provided, I could easily do 20 a year instead of two. I'm shocked when I hear writers expressing difficulty coming up with things to write about. My dental hygienist immigrated from Russia, was a doctor there, is smart, funny, a good storyteller. She has a few books in her. When my co-author Chip Kessler told me about his wife's connection to Dr. Brinkley, the subject of a book, *Charlatan*, I knew instantly there would be a marketing book there, of great interest to my audience. A week's worth of *Wall Street Journals* serves up promising business book ideas. I could do several books just about Disney's marketing, sales, and business strategies, prompted only by studious observation. Life hands over ideas. When I decided to do mystery novels with Les, I had environments in which to place his series' regular detective and other characters: first, behind the scenes in my horse-racing world – the book, *Win, Place Or Die*. Next, behind the scenes in the success industry world, with the chief stage the annual convention of the Global Motivational Speakers Association.

Also, I work with a lot of world-class experts in various complementary fields. I use a lot of co-authors and contributors, much more so now than in early years. They come with ideas. I've never once suffered "writer's block", by the way. Mostly because of the process I described earlier, my piles write my books for me.

What have been your biggest challenges with writing, publishing, and marketing your books?

I imagine the same as most authors: the stunning stupidity of publishers. Their entire business model is tragically dumb. They have no idea of how to sell books. My least-worst publisher, Entrepreneur Press, does a solid job with book production and with distribution, notably via Barnes & Noble and Amazon, and they and my agent do a solid job with international edition and translation edition publishing. They *can* produce and print and distribute books. But they are not so strong when it comes to marketing them. And other publishers are even worse. Fortunately, I realized this early, so I took and take all the responsibility for sales into my hands. I have, as I said, no challenge with writing. None with publishing – I've only had one book I've wanted to do that I've been unable to find a publisher for, and for the past 15 years I've had publishers in waiting. I am also very capable of self-publishing and, circumventing normal distribution, selling 15,000 to 25,000 copies of a book. It would definitely be *nice* to work with a really smart publisher, committed to properly supporting and marketing a book. But my experience and comparison conversations with many authors, including big name, best-selling authors, tells me that is fantasy. I stopped looking for such a publisher and relationship and, instead, concentrated on establishing *my own system* for selling a satisfactory number of each new book and for keeping backlist titles alive over years, into which I could plug each new book – with whatever sales are driven by the publisher's advertising, marketing, or promotion "gravy."

How important are the title and cover to your book sales?

Titles are, for the most part, at least important, in some cases, critical, and God knows I've had to fight publishers for titles built to sell. Many a viable book has been doomed by a dumb title. Titles and subtitles should clearly convey what the book is about, and be more written like headlines and sub-heads for direct-response ads than as literary contrivances. In the business and success genres where I live, a book like the original *Psycho-Cybernetics* and the edition I co-authored, *The New Psycho-Cybernetics*, is an aberration that should not be emulated. All editions combined have sold over 30-million copies, but more despite than because of the title. The reliable formula can be found in almost all the other giant and enduring bestsellers: *Think And Grow Rich; How To Win Friends And Influence People; How I Raised Myself From Failure To Success In Selling; Closing The Sale; The Power of Positive Thinking*. Every one of those titles passes a simple test: would it work as the headline of an ad instead of the title of a book?

Personally, I like injecting something provocative or something waving to a target audience in my titles. In *No B.S. Guide to Ruthless Management of People and Profits*, the word 'ruthless' is there to be provocative. In *No B.S. Time Management for Entrepreneurs*, that "for" is meant to differentiate from hundreds of other books on time management. To say: <u>NOT</u> FOR YOU, if you are a drone, a desk-bound manager or bureaucrat, a schoolteacher, etc. This is important because I am *fishing* with my books and am not interested just in selling the greatest number of books possible, which is why bestseller lists have not been a priority. I want to attract appropriate customers for GKIC and clients for me, that will have significant value, and to resonate with them it's best to repel inappropriate customers. As I mentioned earlier, I have never been interested in being famous on a mass or public scale. Kim Kardashian is welcome to it. I have worked to be what I call 'a famous person nobody has heard of', so, at an event for my audience, 1,000 people will stand in line for photos and autographs, but I can stroll through the hotel lobby utterly ignored. Most of my books are written, published, and promoted with this objective: to create, grow, and sustain fame and influence with a narrow and highly valuable target audience, but be ignored by everybody else.

In a few cases, with other books, fishing is not the chief purpose and titles are broader. In a few cases, the publisher wins a title debate by contract – were it up to me, *The Ultimate Sales Letter* would not be that book's title.

I think chapter titles and subtitles are also very important. Skimming the Contents pages or flipping through a book, a potential buyer is affected by these, and later a buyer is motivated to read or not by these. They are advertising headlines for their chapters.

Covers are a separate issue. They can matter a lot, at retail, on the shelf or the virtual shelf (Amazon, BN.com). We have a set look for all the books in the *No B.S.* series, and only colours and sizes of type vary from one front cover to the next. Outside the series, my covers vary widely. The cover for *Making Them Believe: The 21 Lost Secrets of Dr. Brinkley-Style Marketing* has a distinctive, turn of the century medicine look and colour scheme in keeping with its subject matter.

The issues with all of this are: 1. Differentiation or separation from everything else in the market in your genre – how does your book's appearance stand out from others? 2. Consistency – does the appearance fit the content and author's personality? 3. Audience – does the appearance work for the intended audience? Covers are, I think, more important for fiction than for non-fiction because the book is being bought for entertainment rather than for information.

Having said all that, it is all of much, much less importance than the marketing for a book because the number of books that sell themselves off shelves to browsers is shrinking by the day. There are way, way too many books published with most getting little or no marketing because publishers are business and marketing idiots and authors are delusional. Best title and cover on earth is no better than the worst if it sits spine out on a shelf or is never seen by its potential buyers.

What do you do to promote your books? What are your favourite book marketing strategies?

I have an established system into which each book is inserted. It includes a mix of paid advertising, very targeted publicity, and pushing it out to the informal network of hundreds of niche-industry information marketers I've put in orbit around me, each of whom has their own little yet mighty offline and online media platform reaching several thousands of business owners who respect their recommendations. The best time to build such a network for yourself was 10 years ago, but the worst time is never. If you go look, for example, at GreatLegalMarketing. com, you'll find an information marketing, training, and coaching organization working only with lawyers. There are similar businesses in accounting, banking, financial services, chiropractic, dentistry, auto sales, home furnishings sales, interior decorating, restaurants, retail, etc., etc., and I maintain relationships with them all so that they will, when called upon, recommend, review, excerpt from or even teach from my next book. Linked to this, is the way I engineer a book to start with, which I described earlier. That sets up automatic, guaranteed promotion.

I also tend to devote from one to three days per book to doing tele-seminars, telephone and recorded interviews, sometimes webinars mostly with some of these same industry thought leaders, but also with selected talk radio programs and print media. All this is crammed into one, two, or three days, 20 minutes for this, 30 for that, back to back, with few breaks, from 7 a.m to 4 p.m. I have at different times also employed a retired journalist to pursue trade journals in hundreds of fields, getting book chapters turned into customized articles placed and promoted. I've held book signings at retail locations, and on two occasions, gotten a sponsor (Infusionsoft, the leading direct marketing software company) for a 4-Cities-In-4-Days Tour. There, I spoke at a bookstore and set up shop to sell my books and autograph them at events in L.A., Phoenix, New York, and Orlando. With the *No B.S.* books, the publisher provides one full-page ad in *Entrepreneur Magazine,* other advertising at their dot.com sites, e-zines, etc., and arranges for dedicated emails and other promotion with Amazon. Co-authors often do more active work with *Entrepreneur* than I do, and are more willing and available than I for randomly scheduled media interviews.

I have no favorite strategies. There are some that work for other authors that I refuse to use because they are too time-consuming or reach too broad of an audience (people I am not interested in attracting). But bookselling, particularly business bookselling, is about small numbers multiplied, not about one big thing, so my system interweaves a lot of activities and investments.

How do your e-book sales compare with physical paperbacks?

Each year, e-book numbers creep up as a percentage of total sales. This helps fiction writers far more than business writers like me, and it bites into royalty income. A lot of my books are now sold via Kindle. Fortunately, many followers buy both the e-book edition and a hard copy. People still buy two, three, six, thirty, fifty hard copies to distribute as gifts or to clients. I prefer having people buy physical books; the books are more useful to them because they can use highlighter, Post-It notes, corner fold, and the physical book buyer is a more valuable customer or client going forward. By far, the most valuable client for me is the person who left his house, got in his car, drove to a bookstore, had a subject in mind, browsed, discovered me in that outing, invested in one or several of my books, took them home, read them and responded to offers in them.

Amazon itself is a boon, of course, particularly with people already looking for me by name, because when they get there, I'm never out of stock, invisible, or represented only by a couple titles – *everything is always there*. The e-books are especially helpful to buyers beyond U.S. borders, where physical copies may be hard to find and troublesome to get shipped. Last year, 2014, was the first year that total sales of the trade published books hit about a 50-50 mark: 50% physical, 50% digital.

What has this added to the bottom line of your business?

Books were a major driver of the newsletter/membership business from the beginning, as I built it, through the years it was Glazer-Kennedy Insider's Circle and owned by Bill Glazer, and still are today, in its GKIC incarnation with its private equity and corporate owners. The business is all about two things: *member acquisition* and *member retention*, and as I described earlier, my books serve both purposes. You probably know the Christmas movie *It's A Wonderful Life*, in which an angel shows Jimmy Stewart's character how everyone else's life would have been had he never lived and been a part of it all. Had my books never been, I'd speculate the business would be less than one-quarter of its size, my own wealth similarly dwarfed, and building it would have been much costlier – essentially, customers and clients come free of cost via the books.

Total customer value in the GKIC business, back-end, ranges from a low of $720.00 a year to, more commonly, over $4,000.00 a year, to as high as $45,000.00 a year. About 5% of all customers are members for life with 5 to 30 years tenure, and there is a large contingent we informally call "$100,000 Club", who have invested over $100,000 in the business' products, courses, events, coaching, and services. Those numbers tell you that each individual brought through the front door matters a lot – in fact, just one good customer-member acquired by first discovering and reading one of my books can be worth more than the total royalties from the book's sales life!

The books are also very effective *fishermen*, a fleet of them that bring me very valuable private consulting, coaching, and copywriting clients. My first paid speaking engagements came as direct result of books in the marketplace. Consulting clients leapt to me very recently as direct result of first encountering my books on Amazon. Others migrate to me, originating with books, then through gestation in GKIC membership. I do about $1.5 million a year in personal income from consulting and copywriting, and about one-third of that has direct linkage to my books.

So, the contribution to bottom-line is very substantial. And not as you posed the question, as "added to", but as the foundation and integral driver.

Tell me a little about GKIC for readers who'd like to know more.

GKIC publishes six different monthly, print, paid subscription business newsletters, two monthly audio programs and a comprehensive portfolio of print and digital courses and resources on a wide range of marketing and business subjects. It conducts two major convention-type conferences and a handful of other seminars during the year and operates three group-coaching programs. It is, in short, a business publisher. Second, because it operates on a membership model, it is the largest international association of direct marketing oriented entrepreneurs, business owners, private practice professionals and sales professionals. It is also a trading and joint venture platform for countless vendors, service providers, and experts. It began as me with my own newsletter, and was initially chiefly built by my speaking and by my books. It has grown from tiny to a multi-million dollar a year enterprise owned by a private equity group. I have been under contract to it the most recent dozen years or so as a chief content provider and author, strategic advisor, and speaker at its events.

Summary for Super-Busy Entrepreneurs

- Publish or perish: your business needs a book if it is to thrive.

- You don't need to be *inspired* to write a book. It is a *pragmatic* decision for business purposes.

- Most experts have a "positioning book". This establishes you as an important and authoritative leader in your field.

- Use your book to secure consulting and speaking engagements.

- Each book should have an "eco-system" attached to it to generate money. This can be integrated into a bigger eco-system of income streams.

- A book is the best means of being discovered by the best customers for your business.

- Never face a blank page. Gather raw material and organise it into piles for each chapter. Eventually, shuffle this into a sensible order.

- Calculate the minimum hourly income required for your time and let this dictate the number of hours a book can be given.

- Write in an environment where there are no distractions or interruptions, i.e. without the Internet or in a room without windows.

- Write to benchmarks, deadlines, and the clock.

- Have a defined persona. Don't wander off and do something inconsistent.

- Include case studies that demonstrate your teaching. Charge a promotional fee to be included or ask them to buy quantities of the book or help to promote it.

- You can triple your royalty income through promotional fees. It also establishes promotional support in advance of publication.

- Many publishers have no idea how to sell books. Take responsibility for all your book sales into your own hands.
- Dumb titles doom books. Your title should read like the headline of an advert rather than as a literary contrivance.
- Chapter titles are important and can motivate a potential buyer to read or not.
- Your book cover should be consistent with your book contents and your personality and your audience.
- Devote two or three days to doing teleseminars or webinars or print media to promote your book.
- Business book selling is about small numbers multiplied, not about one big thing.

TONI MASCOLO, OBE

"He gave a copy of my book to the Queen."

Toni Mascolo, OBE, opened his first hairdressing salon with his brother in 1963.

Toni&Guy is now the world's most successful hairdressing business. It employs around 8,000 staff and has an annual turnover of around £175 million generated from over 480 salons worldwide.

Famous clients have included: David Beckham, Diana Ross, Gregory Peck, Andrew Lloyd Webber, Dusty Springfield, and the Rolling Stones.

Toni&Guy was one of the very first hairdressers to introduce innovative "look books" for clients who came to their salons. Toni is also author of *Toni: My Story* (published in 2015), which tells the poignant rags-to-riches story of his business.

The Toni&Guy Charitable Foundation has supported many projects. These include: a children's ward at King's College Hospital in London, MacMillan Cancer Support, The Stroke Association as well as a hostel and apartments for those in need in a church-run project in southern Italy.

I must have been about 12 when I started. I was doing perms for my dad in Italy. So, at Christmas time, I used to do hundreds of those perms: winding them and putting on the silver foil, and then they get hot, and then you take them out. So I did that. My father did lots of competitions; he used to take me everywhere with him. He was very proud for me to be there with him. Around that age, I remember going to this big hairdressing competition, and my dad came up to me and said, "I don't know what I'm going to do with you, you're such a shy little boy. Go and introduce yourself to the president of the committee. Tell them who you are, you're Franco Mascolo's son." And I said, "Nah I'm okay." "No, no, you have to go and introduce yourself." So I had to go and shake hands and say, "I'm Franco Mascolo's son," and he said, "Oh, that's very good, thank you."

I was quite good in grammar school. I did five years of Latin, two years of Greek, French, and all those types of subjects. My cousin was a professor of mathematics, and he was helping me with my studies. So after that, I left Italy when I was 14 and a half. My father had three or four salons: one in Salerno, one in Scafatti, one in Poggiomarino and one in Pompeii – they were all over the place. But then he got an offer to move to London.

My mother had never travelled in that part of the world, and she didn't speak English. So, at that particular time, she forced herself. She felt it was her duty to go with her husband. So they moved to England with four kids – four boys – when I was 14. I was thinking, 'Great, I'll go to London and start a new life; new things and everything else.' Little did I realise that I was done with my five years of grammar school.

I was doing well at school. I had jumped a couple of classes because, in Italy, you can jump, or you can go down – you've got to pass before you move on. So, I was a couple of years away from university.

When I arrived in England, I couldn't speak English, and my mother couldn't speak English. I tried to translate everything from Italian to English, and I had a heck of a job because you can't translate the meanings of everything. My brothers were younger. After one year, they could speak English as well as anybody, because they just learned.

So, when I moved to London, my father said, "You might as well help me doing hairdressing," because I couldn't carry on with my studies in English. I remember at one point my dad said to me, "Come on, you've been helping me to do perms. Look, that lady wants a shampoo and set. You do it." I said, "I've never done it before." So he said, "Don't be stupid: you can do it." Then I did her hair – setting it, maybe like the Queen has her hair, Italian style or something like that – and I thought, 'That was simple to do. It was easier to do than I thought,' so then I moved on. I then started practicing razor cutting; I found it very easy and very artistic.

At that time, I used to work for a hairdresser called Viccari. It's not there any more. But it was a very, very interesting place. We had Christopher Lee, Alfred Marks, who used to come there. I was introduced to Charles Forte, and he gave me a £1 note as a tip and said to me, "I hope this is the start of your career." You probably remember Malcolm Muggeridge, the editor of *Punch*, he was there too. He gave Mr. Viccari a cheque for £1 million, but unfortunately, he put the date of 2050! So it was a fun place to work.

I got a lot of experience – I did a lot of perms and colours, and learned to be very quick with brushing and things. So suddenly, I became a hairdresser from someone who was meant to become maybe a lawyer or something like that. But that's just how it was. After this, I moved to Stockwell and worked for Gerrards and then to Lorenzo's in Victoria Street where we had clients such as Barbara Castle; I did her hair because my boss was getting too old! I also looked after Mrs. May who was the wife of the secretary of the Prime Minister Sir Alec Douglas Hume, and she asked me to go for tea in Downing Street at the age of 18! Sir Alec was in Scotland so Mrs. May's husband showed me the cabinet room. Funnily enough my Toni&Guy salon in Victoria today is on Victoria Street in the same shop as Lorenzo's!

At that particular time, I had one thing in my mind: to buy my mother a house. So I worked hard: I started at eight in the morning and finished about nine or ten at night. I worked five full days, and then on the Saturday half-day, instead of leaving I would stay 'til about six in the evening. Fortunately, I had some of my best years and I saved up enough to buy my mother a detached little house. In today's money, it would probably be quite a lot. That detached house might even be worth half a million now.

At that time, my mother was looking after five of us. My brother was working at a salon in Craven Park Road, and I thought that I really wanted to stay where I was. I was happy. So I was working for Lorenzo's. But, my father wanted to set up a hairdressing business together. He said, "You come with the family, and we'll do it together." So I went to work with my brother Guy. We did "Roman Elegance" and "Florentine" and "Venetian". I can't remember all those adjectives now, but in other words there was Italian elegance. My father joined us, and said, "We'll start Mascolo and Sons Ltd.," because it's good when you start a company. So that's how we started. Then, we thought, 'Well maybe it's the time to call it something else. So I thought I'd like to have a little bit of an Italian family look and feel. So, eventually, we started Toni&Guy, and that was the name that we had.

We started in 1963 in Clapham and worked very hard. We had a very cold winter I remember; it was one of the coldest ever. By Christmas Eve 1964, we had this small little shop and customers would come up and say "hello" to you. It was a great place to work. There was myself, Guy, my father was helping us as well, and there was the assistant, Pauline, who eventually became my wife. The original girls all left – I don't think they were very keen on Italians – so, unfortunately, no one stayed other than Pauline.

Guy did I think 64 clients in one day, and I did 59 – it was like doing a show! That's including perms and everything else; highlights, the lot. And my wife, Pauline, used to do beehives on top, curls on top, and I think she did 29. But mind you, her 29 probably would have been more like 80 of mine because she was incredibly quick, and the shape that she created was just unbelievable, and wouldn't exist this day anywhere. You could have the best hairdresser in the globe, and he wouldn't get anywhere near doing that.

So your work has brought you into contact with many famous people, including royalty.

I met Mr. Lavarini [founder of London's Spaghetti House] at my house, and I know that he gave a copy of my book to the Queen.

Over the years, I've also met Princess Anne and the Duke of Edinburgh.

Excellent. There can't be many authors whose books have been read by the Queen!

So, getting back to Toni&Guy: my brother Guy was a very good hairdresser, the Toni&Guy artistic team won hairdressing awards at the British Hairdressing awards 11 times in a row. We won so many championships that we felt, 'It's not right that there's no competition for anyone else.' So after 11 years, we stopped. Then, we had the opportunity to cut hair for the actress from *The Avengers*, Joanna Lumley. We designed her hair for her role as Purdey in the television show.

Tell me about your "look books" where you have hairstyles and new looks for your customers. You were one of the first hairdressers to have these.

Yes, we did our first book in about 1973. We got the inspiration because we used to advertise in *Ms London* and *Girl About Town,* and this proved to be very popular with our clients, and we were totally fully booked, so much so that another hairdresser close by said that he took our overflow and made so much money that he moved to America! Our first book was called *Hair* by Toni&Guy. We've done so many of them now. We have a team assemble them and put them together. We have over 30 books in the series. There are others as well. Here's our current book.

So this is a full-colour, glossy "coffee table" book – it looks very high quality and glamorous. And you've produced over 30 of these. What sort of impact have these had on your business?

We did them because of education, education, education. We started with our first training academy in St Christopher's Place, and that really built us up to the next level. Before this, we used to have a small school, which was underneath our Davies Street salon, and we had six students.

So your full-colour "look books" were targeted at your customers who were coming to have a haircut. Are they targeted at your students too?

They're targeted to everyone: clients, students, but we have also created another book just for the students.

So you've got a completely different set of books for your students?

Yes. So that's here. We have our *Future Foundation* book series, which is more like a step-by-step guide that teaches the students how to cut, and that literally takes them step-by-step. So these are like the core haircuts of Toni&Guy. Our collection book images are created by our international artistic team, and from all of our hairdressers from Toni&Guy salons all over the world sending their images, it's like a bible of creativity!

So you have several series of books linked to your business with different target readerships. Do you have much input on the production? Or

do you just have the final say when the finished product comes to you?

It's all done in house. My daughter, Sacha, is global creative director, so she heads it all up. She can do all this because she's very experienced. She started working with the company at a very young age, she worked at London Fashion Week, and then she did many shows around the world. She does all the collaborations that we have, with all the designers. Even at the age of 16 or 17, she went to places like Paris and Los Angeles with designers such as Calvin Klein and did the hair for 30 models with one of our assistants.

And then we started doing hairdressing videos. The videos were VHS, Betamax. We were ahead of our time. We had the tapes, but we didn't have enough machines, so obviously we couldn't sell them easily. The demand was so high that there weren't enough machines. We had to do it in NTSC, which was the American system. Then, we went to DVD, and now, obviously it's moved to digital. So now, we mainly give one book to the public: the new Toni&Guy Magazine.

Tell me about this other book on the table.

That's the "Super Brands" book. Toni&Guy is the only hairdressing brand in the world to be nominated as a super brand 10 times. So we're in this book along with other super brands worldwide. Every company that's nominated a super brand gets a copy with their own image and logo on the front. So this has all the other super brands, and Toni&Guy is also in here. We've won about 60 British Hairdressing Awards and over 100 product awards. We've also been nominated as a "CoolBrand" about six times as well.

So how does it feel seeing Toni&Guy in all these books over and over again? Does it ever lose its novelty?

It never loses its novelty, and I am so proud at what Toni&Guy has achieved.

You have a hectic business schedule. Where did you find time to write your book in all of this?

Well, I wrote my book together with my PA, Michelle. I mean it's all my words, everything. But when you speak on the machine with a ghostwriter, you can't always be totally clear. And obviously, my first language is not English, so my grammar is not 100% perfect.

So you recorded it in English rather than Italian?

Yes, in English. I had a ghostwriter who wrote it for me, but it was all my words, it came from the heart. You know, you've got to give the passion, the heart, and the feeling.

Your memoir, *Toni: My Story* goes right back to your early childhood, doesn't it? What inspired you to write your book in the first place?

I remember a lot of things from my childhood. These were good memories, and I remember every little thing. I also have diaries of the things that happened later in life.

I wanted to write a book about my life, where I came from, what I did, and also to leave something for the future. I'd like to write a second book because I wanted to continue with the second part of my mission. Who knows?

Summary for Super-Busy Entrepreneurs

- Make the most of every opportunity to give your book out – even via a friend or acquaintance – to ensure your story is remembered. You never know where your book will end up!

- Consider having different types of books with different goals and different target readerships.

- Use your in-house team of experts, or a ghostwriter, to create your books if you don't have time, or outsource if your business is smaller.

- Create an annual or monthly series to extend the life of your book and keep the content current and up to date.

- A picture speaks a thousand words: your book doesn't have to have lots of text.

- Use high-quality pictures to showcase your talent, skills, and expertise. Glossy full-colour pictures are especially aspirational. They will also whet a customer's appetite for your services.

- Consider creating an educational manual. Use your book to educate new students if your business has a training school or franchises.

- Consider creating a practical step-by-step guide to train students in your methods and give them visual prompts.

- Invite contributions from your staff and ask them to send in pictures of their best work or products. This helps create a sense of community and a shared vision within a large global brand.

- Use on-the-job photos to illustrate how your team works, as well as using more formal images staged by an art team.

- Dictate your book and then transcribe the recording if you have a busy schedule.
- Don't worry if your grammar isn't 100% perfect or English is your second language.
- A ghostwriter can edit your work, but they won't necessarily insert the same heart, passion, and feeling that you will. You'll still need to make a book your own.
- Your personal story with all its highs and lows can be used to inspire others.
- Write a book to honour the past and leave a legacy for future generations.

RICHELLE SHAW

"My book came out six months ago, and we've already booked over half a million dollars worth of business from it."

Richelle Shaw is the leading expert and authority in building successful million dollar businesses. Her experience comes from building her first telephone business to $36 million, losing it all after the 9/11 World Trade Center tragedy, then successfully rebuilding her million-dollar company in approximately five months. As the only female African American public utility owner in the USA, Richelle has won many national awards including Top Woman Entrepreneur of the Year in 2010 and Unstoppable Woman for the Women's Leadership Counsel.

After writing her first book, *How to Build A Million Dollar Business in Las Vegas* (2017), Richelle set on a journey to help entrepreneurs build their own million-dollar businesses. She is also the author of *The Million Dollar Equation* (2012) and *The Million Dollar Equation for Doctors* (2015).

I wrote my books basically because my goal is to really help a million people build million-dollar businesses. Because I know that if I can do that, then I can really change the world. As a little girl, I always said, "I want to make an impact. I want to change the world. What problems do I want to solve?" And I wanted to make sure that I never had to see people impoverished.

I know what happened when I went from working for a company to having my own business. I only had one job my entire life, one real job. I had little side jobs where people would pay me, but only one where I was hired for a job and I received a paycheck every two weeks. I only had one of those before purchasing the company.

There's only so many people that I can actually talk to and help. Even when I speak across the world I only speak with one goal, and the goal is to get them to understand the equation and for them to go home, implement it, and build their business.

Then I had a baby, and now I have a kid. So how do I make sure that I get my ideas into a million people's hands? I said, "Well, one way is to distribute it as a book."

So you realized the power of writing a book in getting your message out. Can you share your experience of writing your books and what it has been like?

My first book *was How To Build A Million Dollar Business In Las Vegas – Without The Casinos.* So, was it easy? Yes, it was easy because I had no expectations. I just said, "You know what? I just want to get out what's in my head so that I can get it to other people." I wrote the first book in about two weeks. I actually talked it into a recorder and then I had a person transcribe it for me.

So when I wrote my second book, *The Million Dollar Equation,* I did it the exact same way. There are challenges in the book, to say the least. I giggled as I reread it, and I thought, 'What the heck was I talking about then?' There was some loss in the train of thought, and there were some grammatical mistakes, and I spelled some things wrong, and I thought, 'What in the world?' But the thing was, I just wanted to get it out of my head at that time.

Now, over a half a million dollars later, with revenue that has been directly related to my book, $548,600 to be exact. I thought, 'Okay, it doesn't really matter that there were errors in the book. It doesn't really matter that I misspelled Oprah's name because Microsoft Word auto-corrected to *Opera.*' Some people say, "I think you meant *Oprah.* You know, *Winfrey.*" I reply, "Oh, okay. Yikes!" And then I look at all the people that got amazing results from reading my book. One of my coaching clients who obtained extraordinary results is actually going to be in the 2nd Edition of The Million Dollar Equation. When we first started working together, he was generating about $80,000 a year all by himself. Last year, he reached

$600,000, and he's on record to reach $2.5 million this year. All of these results are in the last three years since the book's release.

So now, I think, "The book isn't perfect, but it definitely is reaching thousands of entrepreneurs and making an impact." So was it easy? It was easy for me because I had no expectations. It was just an extension of what I was already teaching when I was speaking.

You mentioned to me earlier that you're updating your book *The Million Dollar Equation* right now. Can you explain for my readers what the advantages are of updating a book and what sort of things you are adding in the second edition?

Well, when I wrote the book the first time, it was after I'd already been out of that particular business, so I have some things in the wrong order. For example, one of the things that I tell you to do early on is create your marketing calendar, which basically becomes your action plan. But I realized that it shouldn't be in Chapter 3, it should really be at the very end of the book.

One of the reasons I decided to rewrite the book is because of my own life experiences. I've been teaching, coaching, and speaking for years, but I stepped back a little because I had parents who were sick and a young daughter. I said, "You know what? I think I want to open a consulting agency." So I pulled out my book, and I was going through it and implementing as I was reading the chapters – because, who's the best person to teach you how to build a million dollar business but me? Right? As I started implementing, I was discovering, "Ooh, this chapter's in the wrong place," or "I forgot to add this part." I think when I wrote it originally, I wrote it *after the fact*. This rewrite is all of the things that

I fixed as I was using the book myself, and I found areas where my explanations were incomplete or in the incorrect order.

Now, three years later, I have hundreds more of examples of people who used the process and *The Million Dollar Equation* with amazing results. Some just added an extra $1,000 to their revenue each month, which for them was a game-changer because they were low-income entrepreneurs. Others went all the way up to folks who built multi-million dollar businesses.

So I documented their journey in the second part of the book, which is a lot of fun too, because I think that there are a lot of people who write books from theory and not from practical implementation. As an entrepreneur, I always strive to give people practical implementation and actionable steps instead of just, "in theory, this is what's *supposed to happen.*"

The reason why entrepreneurs give up is if things don't go right, they think that it's an anomaly and that things should be perfect. This is because the theoretical books that you normally read in a bookstand only tell you about the success. They don't tell you about the failures. That's why I think it's really important that I rewrite this book so I can tell them that when they get an extra $1,000 from doing everything right that I told them to do in the book, that is still a success and that they shouldn't give up and should keep going.

You've mentioned featuring success stories in your book of people you've worked with. Sometimes new authors feel a little reticent about asking if somebody would mind their story being included in

their book or perhaps writing a testimonial. What's your experience of this?

Most of them have been so excited about their results that they're excited to be featured. One of the ways that I extended the revenue-generation part of the book is that I created groups and memberships into groups that were free so that all you had to do is buy the book and you could become a member. And so, we highlight several members that are doing great things, and they're excited to be famous even in our little group and to show what they're doing so that they can help others. So I haven't had a problem with people giving testimonials or wanting to be featured.

Now, let's move on to the subject of 'value' and the sales price for the book. You have quite high price points for your books – I think they start around $45. Many authors can get a bit anxious about pricing their books so high and worry they might not sell. Can you explain why it is a good idea to price your book so high?

There's a few reasons. The first is because I wanted folks who were really serious about making a difference in their lives to make the investment. And if it's free, then most people don't take it seriously, and the book would only sit there unread. If you pay $45, you're going to think, 'OK, this means something to me.' So that's number one.

The second thing is that gives me a space to play with the price a little bit and to have sales and to give discounts without it cutting into my revenue. So that's another reason.

The third reason is that it gives me a better customer. I don't want to create a tribe of discounters. That's not fun. Those aren't people who will buy other things later on.

And the fourth reason – and this is I think the key and the biggest reason – is that I'm creating a business, and my book is not the business. What I watch many new authors do is that the book they've created becomes their business, and their only goal is to sell as many as they can. That's what they're going to live off of. And I don't think that's a good idea. It should be that a book is used to enhance an existing business.

My latest book is *The Million Dollar Equation For Doctors*. What sparked me to write it is that I have an existing consulting business that consults only with physicians. The challenge was that they would read my other book *The Million Dollar Equation,* a book that's for the general business owner, and not understand how it applies to their own business. So I wrote my latest book as a way to get leads – for them to see that, number one, I was the authority, and then number two, so that they would say, "I need your agency to help me run my practice."

So the business is not the book; the book is just a bonus. The book is just a positioning key and a way for me to lead them into a consulting relationship. I see that a lot of people missed that point, in that they will say, "How can I sell as many books as possible?" Then, they're stuck because they've created a business that has only one product, and that's it. So what can you do in order to make more money? You have to write a new book. Whereas I get a lot more longevity out of my existing books because I create the book as a complement to my existing business.

You make some great points there. You've mentioned positioning yourself as an expert and attracting certain types of clients. What I often hear from authors is, "I can't write about that topic because I'm not a doctor" or whatever. So they steer clear of subjects unless they have direct experience. Tell me more about your decision to write about *The Million Dollar Equation For Doctors* even though you're not a doctor yourself.

Well, I'd been consulting with them for eight years. So, no, I'm not a doctor, and I don't pretend to be, but what I do understand and what I am an expert in is building a business. And I happen to believe that no business is different. I don't care if it's a medical practice or if we're selling daisies at a corner flower shop.

There's only three ways to grow a business. Number one: get new customers. Number two: get your existing customers to come back more often. Number three: get your existing customers to spend more per transaction.

Let's say you're at the market, and as you're about to check out, there's lots of stuff at the front of the store. So there's gum, there's candy, there's magazines, there's the tabloids – all of those things will increase your transaction size. So, if you come into the market, and you're only there to get a bottle of water, you end up getting candy. They've increased your transaction. So that's the way that they grow.

I don't care what kind of business you are. If you're a medical practice, there's still only three ways to grow. You have to get a new patient, get your patient to come back more often, or sell more to your existing patient while they're there. So I had to learn new terms and talk about,

"Well, let's figure out what else is ailing our patient when they come to see us," instead of they're just focusing on the headache. Well, what else is wrong with them that's creating the headache? And then now we can prescribe to fix *all* of the things that are wrong with the patient.

But, theoretically, there's only still three ways. So once I started working with physicians and going into their businesses and applying the same things that I applied in my telephone business to their medical practice, it worked. That's when I got confirmation that, "You know, this is crazy! It's exactly the same principles."

Now, when I talk to new prospective clients that are physicians or when they read the book, they understand. So I say, "Okay, nobody taught you how to run a business in medical school, but I'm going to teach you the fundamentals of Business 101 and then we're going to apply these things to your medical practice." When I explain it that way, they say, "Oh, my goodness, nobody ever told me that. Well, that's why I keep adding staff because we keep having to see more patients. But we're seeing the wrong type of patients instead of seeing the right type of patients." Well, all that is, is about having the right target market.

Let's move on now to the subject of book covers. *The Million Dollar Equation* and *The Million Dollar Equation For Doctors* have a similar kind of branding to each other. They're both quite simple in design, aren't they? Whereas your first book *How To Build A Million Dollar Business In Las Vegas* is much busier, and you also have your photo on the front. Tell me more about your covers and how you chose them.

Sure. When I wrote the first book, there was no goal to the book. It was autobiographical, and I shared stories of other people that were here in our local community. At the time, I was building a local following here where I could teach people the marketing strategies and coach them and get clients. So my goal was just to become the authority in my local market, and that's why it's Las Vegas themed – the colours are pretty Las Vegas colours – and I put myself on the cover thinking that that would be a really good thing. From that book, I actually tallied it, and it was somewhere around $30,000 of revenue that I generated from that book.

So when I wrote my second book, *The Million Dollar Equation,* I felt first of all that my title was way too long. I needed a catchy title; I needed to name the thing that I was doing. So in *How To Build A Million Dollar Business,* I was telling the stories, but I didn't give a lesson with each story.

We all know that from speaking: we tell a story to give the lesson, and we never give a lesson without telling a story. So I became a better writer the second time around. Then, I wanted to take myself off of the cover and really depersonalize it the second time, so that's why my cover is very simple for *The Million Dollar Equation.*

Then, when I wrote my third book, *The Million Dollar Equation For Doctors*, the original title was *MD Incorporated.* And I said, "Okay, well that makes sense. Oh, I love this title." I was walking around, talking about *MD Inc.* this and *MD Inc.* that. But then, I realised, "Hold on a second. I already have an established brand that is all about building a million-dollar business. That's been my common thread. That's what sets me apart from everybody else. So why wouldn't I just call it *The Million Dollar Equation For Doctors*? Doesn't that make sense?"

So I went back to the same designer and said, "Okay, let's have the same feel for the second book, but let's use a different graphic." That's when we picked the dollar sign with the stethoscope so that it would make a little bit more sense. But that's the reason why I went for a simpler cover – and I also was looking at who my market was. The first time, it was local; I didn't think I needed it to be as sophisticated. This last time, it needed to be a little bit more sophisticated because I was going to the physician market.

So, when I look at the cover, what is going through my head is, "Do I have the right title?" And I test that often. I test it not only by just asking people, but I test it using some online strategies. I will survey my list. I will survey other folks to see how they feel about it. I will start using it in previews to see if I get any negative reaction where people go, "What's that all about?" Whereas when I did *The Million Dollar Equation For Doctors*, everybody got it right away. Because they said, "Oh, okay. We're just taking *The Million Dollar Equation* and extending it."

So I do lots of research beforehand, and I'm not afraid to make changes at the last minute. The book cover for *The Million Dollar Equation* had a guy running up steps originally, but right before I launched it, I changed it to the green cover that it has now. For *The Million Dollar Equation For Doctors,* I had picked a white cover originally. But when I got the preview, I thought, "You know, white covers can get all messed up, and then they don't look really great." Plus, I didn't fall in love with it. So I went back to a blue cover, got another preview copy, and then I just stayed with it.

Well, as we both know, writing and publishing a book are just two parts of an author's journey. So let's explore what you did to promote your books. Share with me some of the promotion you've done such as hosting a book launch, doing book readings, signings, and tours.

Well, yeah, I had to do all of those things. One of the things that I had decided is that I wanted to go and do the whole book launch. There were a lot of people online, selling services to you. When I investigated, I asked, "Okay, what's the return on investment?" – you know, I'm a business person. And they answered, "You won't make your money back from the launch." I was surprised: "I won't?" They replied, "No, no. This is just about letting folks know you're out there and getting your name out there. Isn't that great? You'll be famous!"

So I said, "I don't want to be famous. First of all, I want to impact as many people as possible, so I don't know if that's really the right direction for me." So I did my own launch in my own way. I contacted some folks who would be happy to be an affiliate for me – who liked me, who believed in me, who believed in what I was doing – and they came and said, "You know what? We'd love to promote it for you."

I did hundreds of podcasts. I mean, literally hundreds of online seminars and webinars. I did tons myself during the process, and it all just worked. From the promotion that I did myself, I got booked to speak at other events, and so we were shipping books there. Then one of the things that I did (which is what I recommend all folks who write books should do) is I created one sheet that I would send to different organizations, saying, "Okay, here's the deal: I will waive my speaking fee, which is normally $5,000 to $10,000, if you just guarantee to buy 100 books."

So they would guarantee to buy 100 books. Sometimes they'd have 300 or 400 people there, and they would buy the books. Of course, I got the books wholesale so that would cover my expenses, and they had to pay for me to fly there back and forth. But, I think I got eight groups to take that deal within the first year of the launch. Then, while I was there, naturally what happens is the person who has the book asks you to sign it, and then they want people to purchase other things too.

Great strategy. Tell me more about your podcasts. Many new authors think that they should really only cover the topics in their books when they're doing a promotion.

You know what? I talked on a variety of different themes. The majority were business-building, but there were some things that were like, "How do you manage being a mom and being an entrepreneur?" and "How do you manage schooling your kids?" I went to anybody who I could possibly make the connection with, looking at what made me stand apart from other people and what made me great. There are thousands and thousands of podcasts, and I would just pitch it.

Let me explain one of the things I definitely did differently from some other folks. When I first bought the telephone company, I hired a PR firm, and I was paying them $10,000 a month to get in the press. This was because I thought that as soon as people heard about me, that they would be flooding the telephone company with calls.

Well, it didn't work out that way at the end of the day. So I have three stories of me in local press. My mother has them up on the walls of the house so that you can be all impressed. It's pretty, but it didn't give me any customers. So what I had to figure out was, "Okay, so, why do I need this and what for?" So I became my own PR pitch machine, and I figured out how to pitch myself so that when I talked to the media, I'd say, "Hi. I'm the only female African-American public utility owner in the nation. Wouldn't you love to have me on your show or at your event?" Or, "How can I help you? Here are the three ways that I think that I could help your audience." And they would call me back and say, "You know what? I think that's great! Yeah, yes. We're having you."

That's how I have my local television segment that I do three times a month, because I pitch the media and tell them: "This is what I do." And it has nothing to do with business. I do consumer reports most of the time, 'How to find the best travel' or segments of 'How you can make money' and 'How you can save money.' But it's nothing directly connected to 'How to grow a business.' It was because it was one of those ideas that I pitched in the first place, and now, four years later, I'm still on the show.

This is something I've been saying for a long time. Authors don't need to pay out lots of money for PR – they can do it themselves if they learn to pitch correctly. That's not to say it will always be plain sailing. There will always be challenges along the way won't there?

Yeah, yeah. I made a lot of mistakes. The first book I wrote was the wrong book to write because I didn't write it to make money. So I had to figure out like, "What's your goal?" with my later books. So when I wrote my next book, *The Million Dollar Equation,* I wrote it basically in modules so that, "Here's the first thing you do; here's the second thing you do." And then I made videos of each module, and then sold the modules.

So that's how I was able to make half a million dollars off one book. I didn't sell three million copies, and I'm not a New York Times bestseller, but I was able to create a book that made money for the regular, everyday person. So I figured out, "Okay, I can't do it the traditional, old-fashioned way. I have to do it with a purpose in mind."

So now with the latest book, *The Million Dollar Equation For Doctors,* it's 1,000 per cent different from *The Million Dollar Equation* because I have a different audience, and my goal is different. My goal is not to sell modules so that they can do online tests. The goal of my latest book is to get clients from it. So it worked for that book too. It's one of those things that I send directly to a doctor's practice, and then they call for a consultation, and then we go in, and we close the sale. So it came out six months ago, and we've already booked over half a million dollars worth of business from it.

A book can be very powerful in generating clients for a business and in closing sales. Of course, this is a very non-traditional way of looking at a book. So what has the wider impact on your business been from writing books?

It's a game changer, definitely. You have to understand that your book is not your business and that you have to build in what they call a proverbial back-end. The book needs to lead them somewhere else rather than just to reading another of your books.

It's changed everything for me, everything. Now people say, "Oh, you're an author!" I laugh because I'm a horrible writer. I murder verbs. I do because I'm an entrepreneur. I'm a go-getter. So I don't follow any rules; I never follow any rules. I'm glad though that I wrote my first book that was awful because it led me to get better and better at it. If there's anybody who's thinking about, 'Oh, should I write a book for my business?' Absolutely. Not only should they write it but just get on and do it. Don't wait to get something right or something perfect. Just do it so that you can get it out there – start fixing it after it's out in the market.

You have to have a tough skin because people are mean and cruel, and they leave some reviews that aren't so nice. But then you also get the other people who say, "That person is crazy. I got so much out of that book. This is one of the best books I've ever read in my life." And I have those reviews too.

Yes, unfortunately, that's one of the downsides of the Internet is that reviewers can say what they like anonymously without much regulation. Finally, you chose to self-publish. Can you share with my readers your reasons for choosing self-publishing rather than a mainstream publisher?

All right. Well, number one, I'm a marketer, so I market for myself every day. That wasn't my life's goal to get published by somebody else. I looked at traditional publishers and found that they were only going to give me a very little amount per book even though I was still required to do the majority of the promotion. So if I am going to do most of the work, then I want $9 and 8 cents from my book instead of 90 cents.

I also wanted to know who was buying my books because what's really important to me is the list of people buying it so I can reach them to tell them about other things.

So you get to keep the names of your readers rather than having the publisher keep them.

Correct. One of my friends had a book deal, and it took her publisher two and a half years to go through the process and finally release it. Now she's doing very well. She's spoken all over the world, and she's done television segments. But her goal was to be a highly sought-after speaker.

So she has all that, but here's her challenge now. She came to me two months ago and said, "Okay, so what do I do now?" Because the book has basically fizzled. I said, "Well, what does your publisher want you to do?" She replied, "They want me to write a new book. But I don't have another book in me." I asked her, "What are you going to do then?"

Now, at all of her events, she's trying to get a list together of people who attend or who read her book. She's coming back to me to ask for help. How does she monetize her book – because she never created the business first? If she doesn't show up to speak, she doesn't get paid. We both have children the same age, and her son hasn't seen her at a school function very often because she's traveling three weeks out of the month.

I feel so badly for her because her success has come at a high price. Success to me means being able to do exactly what I want to do when I want to do it and making money in my sleep. If I don't show up to speak at an event, I still want to make money. I'm also at every event, volleyball game, dance performance. I take my daughter to school each day and pick her up. By creating additional products and services linked to my books, I now have total freedom to live my life enjoying every minute.

And it's also important to you to impact on people's lives. So how many people do you think you've actually reached through your books and your work?

I know it's well over 100,000. Two years ago, I started to count how many people have visited the different websites that I have and opted in, and through my online reach, so I know that it's over 100,000. It's not at 1 million yet, but I know that it will be. And as a little self-published author, I'm really proud of the impact that I've made.

Summary for Super-Busy Entrepreneurs

- There are only so many people that you can talk to and help each day, whereas a book is a good way to get your ideas to a million people.

- Talk your book into a recorder, and have it transcribed, to get your first draft written in just two weeks.

- It doesn't matter if the book is perfect, or if it has occasional grammatical errors if it's making an impact and changing lives.

- Give your readers practical, actionable steps that they can implement instead of just theory.

- Extend the revenue generation of your book by creating membership groups. All readers have to do is buy the book to become a member.

- Feature success stories from people who have benefited from your teachings.

- If your book is given away free or at a low price, it won't be taken seriously or will sit unread.

- A higher-priced book will attract a better quality of client or customer.

- A higher retail price for your book will allow you flexibility for sales promotions and discounts.

- Your book should never become your primary business. It should be a complement to your existing business.

- You don't need to have direct experience of topics you write about. For example, you don't need to be a doctor to write about building a million-dollar medical practise.

- Choose colours and images on your book cover that match your subject and target readership.
- Test the title of your book on potential readers both online and offline. Use surveys to test for positive and negative reactions.
- Don't be afraid to make last-minute changes if something isn't working.
- Be prepared to do podcasts and webinars to promote your book online. These don't necessarily have to be about the topics in your book. They might be about finding the best travel or schooling your kids, for example.
- Ask people who believe in you and what you're doing to promote your book for you.
- Waive your speaking fee in return for a guarantee to buy books.
- Learn how to become your own PR pitch machine. Don't pay $10,000 a month to get in the press.
- Traditional publishers give low royalties even though you do the majority of the promotion, and you also won't know who is buying your books. Consider self-publishing instead.

MARK VICTOR HANSEN

"The story has to give you chilly bumps, a tear in the eye, or move your stomach."

Mark Victor Hansen is the co-author of *Chicken Soup for the Soul,* which is one of the most successful publishing franchises of all time. The non-fiction series has more than 250 titles, with 500 million copies sold in over 54 languages.

Mark's other bestselling books include *The One Minute Millionaire* (2002), *Cracking the Millionaire Code* (2005), *How to Make the Rest of Your Life the Best of Your Life* (2006), *The Aladdin Factor* (1995), *Dare to Win* (1989) and *The Power of Focus* (2000).

Earlier in his career, Mark did labour work for $2.14 per hour after losing over $2 million virtually overnight through a faulty business

decision. However, he bounced back as a speaker for the business market, collaborating with his friend, Jack Canfield on what would eventually become *Chicken Soup for the Soul.*

One of Jack's teachers is Dr. Ken Blanchard who said, "Feedback is the breakfast of champions." I'm a guy who will teach goal setting and self-help forever. I've sold half a billion books. My goal is to sell a billion books. So when we did *Chicken Soup for the Teenage Soul* – which alone sold 19 million of the 500 million books we've sold – we tested it on 12,000 teenagers. We took the name of the co-author and ourselves off, so they didn't know if the stories were written by Mark or Jack or whoever. So they had to judge and evaluate the stories without being influenced in any way.

We started this process 20 years ago and have never changed it. We asked them to judge a story on a scale of one to ten. We said, "Look, if some of the stories touch you and are so memorable you want to retell them, let's call it a ten-plus-plus-plus." To start with, we read 1,000 stories to find one that was good. Then we distilled this down to 250, sent them out to all the kids at Nickelodeon – 12,000 electronic kids that tested it, who were age appropriate. Then, the feedback came back, and a lot of the stories we thought were going to make it didn't make it. They also said, "Listen. You guys don't have to moralize us. You don't have to tell us, "Call your mother."" We thought: "OK. Wow, cool!" So we got plenty of feedback.

With most authors, feedback is very limited. It's the author, maybe his or her spouse, and the editor. We think a broad spectrum of feedback is good. We're accepting of criticism and not critical of ourselves or the people giving it to us. Basically, the story has to have clout. It has to give you chilly bumps, a tear in the eye, or move your stomach. All of a sudden, you might read a story and say, "Wow. I really haven't called my mother or father in the last 20 years. I ought to do that. That's probably a good idea. They're going to die!" Something simple like that. Generally speaking, we do heart-touching, soul-penetrating stories.

So you're testing your ideas first, and your writing has to connect emotionally with your readers.

Yes, because we're emotional beings. We're spiritual, mental, physical, financial, but we're emotional in every one of these dimensions of our humanness. So hopefully our book hit the totality of what we would call being a human, and we found the dimensionality that people wanted. We started with one book, and then we got *Chicken Soup for the Mother's Soul* for Mother's Day, and for the last eight years in a row, we've been number one with that. Even I'm surprised nobody has ever competed with that. But I came up with the idea because I thought, "Gosh, I love my mommy, but what do you get mom? You take her to lunch, or you celebrate her on Mother's Day, and you give her flowers. But what else? Couldn't you give her a story that she'll never forget, and really touch her heart?"

That's lovely – it's a great idea. You've created lots of other books and spin-off products from your first book, such as *Chicken Soup for the*

Teenage Soul **which I bought for my son. You've developed it into all sorts of niched books, targeted at different types of readers.**

Yes. So the *Chicken Soup for the Teenage Soul*, have your son read it out loud to you, and you'll both bond better than ever. That's what we've discovered. We've found 38 principles for success with our books. One is that if you find something that works, do sequels and prequels. Do before and afters. Go deep with it, and see how deep the need is.

I'm often asked, "How do you make a book a bestseller?" Well, I ask every author to start by figuring out the end result. First of all, figure out who you're going to market to. Where is your market? Don't start with writing a book because *you* want it. Write a book that the market needs and desperately wants, right?

Exactly. The road to success wasn't easy, was it? You were famously rejected by 144 publishers, who said: "Anthologies don't sell," somewhere around that figure.

That's the number. They all said, "Hit the road, Jack," and I said, "Look, it's okay if you don't like Jack, but I'm a nice guy." I'm joking of course – Jack is a wonder. He's brilliant, he's funny, he's good looking, he plays guitar, he can sing, he can do all sorts of great stuff. He's a good friend.

So what gave you the courage to keep going when other people would have perhaps given up or tried writing a different book?

Okay, that was my responsibility. I've been selling since I was nine years old. Selling is one of many things I teach along with leadership and motivation and why we've got to have alternative energy. The point is, you've got to make yourself rejection-proof. When somebody rejects you,

you've got to use this four-letter, clean word: N-E-X-T. Just say, "Next! …
Next!" Somebody out there is going to be in alignment with you. Now
for whatever reason, the first 144 people that we saw weren't in alignment
with us.

Later, a lot of them came back, like the chairman of Time Warner, who
said, "I made a mistake on that one!" I said, "Larry, you sure did, but I
still love you!" The good news is that the book industry is very gentle
about the way they say, "No." They write you a letter and tell you, "Sorry,
your book is just not a fit for Time Warner right now."

**I think they all use the same template letter! Now, here's an important
topic: is it possible to make money from a book *without* selling
millions of copies?**

Absolutely. There are all sorts of ways to do it. You can do seminars,
telemarketing, or coaching alongside your book. Bob Allen is one of my
co-authors, and we wrote a whole seven-book money series, three of them
with Bob. We did *One Minute Millionaire* and *Cash in a Flash* and *Cracking
the Millionaire Code*. Bob Allen wrote a book called *The Challenge,* and I
think he sold around 60,000 and made around $5 million with it. Here's
what happened. He said, "Send me to any city and take away my wallet,
and I'll buy a million dollars' worth of real estate in 24 hours. Send me
to the unemployment line. Let me go through the line, and I'll make
sure everybody in the line makes $5,000 within the next 90 days." People
wrote in and said, "I've got this challenge or that challenge," and then he
had a seminar series called *The Challenge.*

The Challenge was not a good title for a book in my opinion. In *The
Guinness Book of World Records*, I'm one of the title-writing kings with

307 bestsellers! So I said, "Bob, for a title that didn't work very well, the book was great!" The principles were brilliant, but I think he just mistitled it.

I think everybody ought to write a book. I wrote a book called *You Have a Book in You*. I want everybody to fast-write a good book that makes money. One of the reasons you want to write a book is to build your business. Because if you're an accountant, a real estate person, a doctor or a lawyer, for example, a book gives you mega-credibility and authority. Then if you sign it for your client or patient, they think, "Oh, my gosh, this is a doctor. He must be the best, or she must be the best because they wrote a book on weight loss and I need to lose 10lb!" Every business needs that.

The trash man wrote a book because of me – he wrote *How to Turn Trash into Cash*. "What a good title," I said. I wrote the foreword to it because it was such a cool title! A garbage man had never written a book about garbage before. Well, the sixth biggest business in the world is garbage. I own a little company that's taking all garbage and turning the liability back into an asset ... it's called a liquid plasma reactor, and it's pretty exciting. We're doing it with big cities, and they cost $100 million dollars each. It's self-funding because we each create five pounds of garbage a day. More than you wanted to know!

It's still a cool story.

I'm of Danish descent. My wife is Danish, and both my parents came from Denmark. The top Danish poet is the Laureate, Piet Hein who says, "What the world needs now is problem solvers galore. Because each problem we solve creates 10 problems more!" If there's a problem, then somebody can figure out the solution. Once he or she figures out the solution, I think it is incumbent upon them to write up the solution so everybody can read it. We're the only species on the planet that can transfer knowledge, and the biggest transference of knowledge is technically through books. Yes, we can do videos and movies, but all of it starts generally with the printed word.

Many successful authors I work with are very aware of the Internet and the competition it poses. How do you feel about it?

I think the Internet is exactly like fire. Fire is great. It can either warm a house or burn it down. Fire doesn't care. The Internet is exactly the same: it does not care. For those of us who know how to use all the new devices and social media, it is great. In your country, my friend Richard Branson is the master maestro at marketing. The guy does cute, crazy, wonderful, adventurous things; he is a master.

I'm pretty masterful at it too. Right now, I have a book called *The Miracles in You* that is due out. I will email somewhere between 10 million and 100 million people in the next nine months, and I think I'll sell 10 million books as a result. I've asked all my colleagues to send out an email. My buddy, Bob Proctor, in Canada will mail over a million people. A lot of people are going to do that for me. And people might go, "Well, you can do it because you're famous." Well no – I was born naked, helpless, and ignorant, the same as everybody else! I just decided to discipline myself and build a lot of relationship capital during my 67 years to work with people like Bob.

You've co-authored with a number of people, on all sorts of projects and books. What are the benefits of writing a book with another entrepreneur?

Well, okay, so I'm in the alternative energy business. I own two of the fastest-growing companies – one of which is NPC, Natural Power Concepts. And the world's biggest commercial solar company is called Principal Solar. Well, the chairman of that is a brilliant genius. We're doing big commercial solar projects, where we do solar farms, so we have clean, green, sustainable energy thanks to some batteries that we've created. His name is Michael Gorton. So he comes to my office and says, "What do you think about electric cars?" I said, "Electric cars are the next thing." I think that a decade from now, everyone will say, "What! Are you an idiot, using an internal combustion car?" Your litre of gas is some crazy number in the UK; ours is about five dollars a gallon. Anyhow, we can do $500 of electricity (which we can do clean, green, with wind, geothermal, tidal and solar), versus 550 petrochemicals for the average person driving 10,000 miles.

So he said, "Would you write a book with me?" I said, "Let's dictate it right now." We dictated it, then wrote it back and forth a couple of times and finished a book. In the book, we say, *"You've got an electric car in your future."* Everybody who has read it has given it away to 10 or 20 people, we're told. We're just doing an electronic book because we're in the energy business, and we want everyone to understand: we don't want you to use a petrochemical car. Carbon was a great way to start the planet. But we can't burn up a process that costs us a 100 million years to build: dinosaur juice.

By the way, I'm on my little pulpit, so I'm sorry. I know you asked about co-authors. My wife Crystal is also a great author by herself. She's written a lot of stuff and is also writing some things with me. I love to write books, but the sales process is a stretch these days because you're right, the Internet works for you or against you. However, if you've got the exact right thing at the right time, the marketplace goes, "We will take it." If you do the videos for YouTube, Google, Google+, Facebook, or any of the social media, who knows which one is going to make it? You have to come up with something wild and wiggy. As I said earlier, Richard Branson is one of the key guys to look at because he keeps pushing the edge of everybody's envelope, and I just love and admire him, and I'm thankful that we're friends.

Anyhow, I love co-authorship. I also love writing alone. But you know, these guys show up like Michael Gorton, and I go, "There's no such book as *You've Got an Electric Car in Your Future*," so we fast-wrote it and got it out. It's going to be a seminal book, we think. Yesterday, Michael called me about something else. We're doing the biggest solar project ever in Egypt, and I said, "Michael, here's my idea: why are *we* promoting the book? Let's have Tesla Motors and other electric car businesses promote it. Why don't we have *them* give away our book to everybody that walks into their showroom?" He said, "Great idea, can you do it?" I said, "I don't have that connection today, but I know they're going to bump into me soon because I've written it down. It's a heck of an idea, isn't it?" So that's what I'm saying: you've got to have surrogate ways to market to that somebody who owns every market.

You've got to write a list of 200 people you need to spend time with, play with, quote, and be expanded by. Everybody I've ever written down manifests, because the spiritual law says: "Write it, make it clear, and it'll be established unto you." So I'll write it down, and somewhere down the line, he and I will befriend each other. It's a given in my mind. He just doesn't know me yet, but he will.

So you mix both online and offline promotion. Do you have a preference for one or the other?

Well, I'm really good at speaking – by the way, that sounds ego-oriented, and I didn't mean to be – but you do 5,000 talks to 6 million people live, and you get pretty good at it, I guess! I love doing it. I love entertaining audiences, being funny and bright and light, hopefully. Overall, the audiences go, "Wow, that's cool. I've got to have this guy's book," and then I've signed books 12 hours at a time afterwards.

That's good, but it doesn't do the numbers I need to do. In America to get to the bestseller list, you've got to sell 30,000 books in one week, and you know, I don't have audiences at 30,000. I've got 500 or 1,000 sometimes. Jack and I pumped our book like crazy. We did media all day long, and then at night we did an average of 1,000 to 2,000 people, and then we'd get an airplane at 11 p.m. and fly to the next place, get up at 6 a.m. in the morning, go on TV, do media again and then another meeting. That isn't available today. You can't pull it like we could back then. So now you've got to do social media and electronic media.

Talking of media, in the past, you've appeared on shows like *Oprah*, *CNN*, *The Today Show*, you've featured in *Time* magazine, in *The New York Times*. Have you got any tips for other authors to get the most out of a media interview?

I've got a ton of stuff I could say, but let me just make it as blatant as I can. Pretend you're interviewing me for the BBC right now. Go ahead, ask me a question about the weather. Ask me any question you want about the weather in England. Go ahead, hit it.

OK. *So what do you think of the weather in England?*

Well, the reason I wrote *Chicken Soup for the Soul* is exactly to tell you how the weather is in your mind because the weather outside is determined by how you feel inside. And that's why everyone buys the *Chicken Soup* books so they feel permanently good, even when it's drizzling, rainy, cold, and you forgot your umbrella.

See how it works? Doesn't matter what you ask, I'm going to turn it into a *Chicken Soup* answer if that's what I'm selling that day. I could do the same thing for my new book, *The Miracles in You.* The reason I wrote this book is that weather is miraculous in England...

So basically authors should prepare beforehand, rehearse, and have sound bites ready?

Absolutely. You shouldn't just rehearse beforehand, but you've also got to have somebody grill you and test you so you're used to it. Because if you do enough media interviews, they're going to try and crush you and ask you stuff like you can't believe.

For example, in my case, I was on the biggest radio show in America, with 50 million listeners, and Rick Dees asked me, "Did you see *Titanic?*" Now, he had met my kids fortuitously because we were at a concert together. I had teenagers, and Rick at the time had teenagers. So he said, "Did you go to *Titanic?*"

"Yeah."

"Did you bring your teenagers?"

"Yeah."

"So what'd you say about the hand in the back of the Rolls Royce?"

Well, of course, you know what Leonardo DiCaprio and Kate Winslet were doing.

Luckily, if you've been in enough interviews, you know to answer a skewering question like that with a question. So I said, "What did *you* tell *your* teens, Rick?" Luckily I'm good at that, but they try to catch you and see if they can melt you down. Some of them get paid for being controversial, and you could have the most non-controversial book in the world and still have somebody try to melt you to see if you have the mental temerity to handle it. "How long have you been beating your wife?" Either way, if you answer it, you're dead!

It's easy to look at someone who is successful and assume they've always had it easy, but it hasn't all been plain sailing for you, has it?

No. You have to fight with the publisher, and you've got to fight with the media. You know, *The New York Times* wouldn't take us at first because they said, "Dr. Hansen, look. Here's the way it works. We do not take multi-authored books." The lady sounded pompous and arrogant. I said, "You're absolutely sure?" She said, "I am sure, sir." I said, "Well, let me show you the book that you *do* take and you *do* have in *The New York Times* list periodically, and that is the Bible." The Bible has 66 books, and if you count Maps, 67. She said, "Okay, you're in next week. You're selling

20,000 a week. You win." And we were number one for the next 58 weeks. You know, you've even got to fight the media to get your airspace even though we were selling more books than anybody. Pretty quickly, we had the top 15 of the 50 books on *USA Today*. So we got in *The Guinness Book of Records*.

Nobody else ever did that. No one ever tried to do the volume and the productivity that we wanted to do. Jack and I are probably workaholics, although we have a great life, both of us. I've got one of the best lives in the world, I think. I love what I do: I'm having fun doing this interview with you right now.

Me too! Tell me about a typical day. Do you work 14-hour days or four-hour days? How do you spend your time?

I read about all the authors that only work a couple hours a day. I was recently in Ernest Hemingway's big house in Florida with my family, and I thought, "Get out of here, Ernest! I'm looking at your library. You couldn't possibly read this much." All the books were broken in the back, and he was writing for just a few hours a day. It depends on what you call "work". I mean that my work is my play at some level. My mind is up even in the middle of the night sometimes, going, "Gosh, you've got to write this. This is the coolest idea you've ever had. This is the way to make it work, and this is the way to get it media, and this is the way to get it going." So my mind is going all the time. But in answer to your question: I would like nine hours sleep a night if I could, but I probably get eight hours. Most of the rest of the time I'm working.

But you know, we have a lot of fun. When we do go on vacation, we shut down. We don't bring our cell phones, we don't bring our computers, and we disengage. Because writers – the ones I've met anyhow, including you – tend to burn out once in a while. It's so easy to get excited about a writing project, and then all the sudden you come up with the PR, and you go, "Wow, we should do this and this and this." Then pretty soon, it owns you rather than you own it. So the goal is what Christ said: "Be *in* the world, but not *of* it." Well, that's hard because the book business can suck up your life. You've got to meet other authors, you've got to meet agents, you've got to meet the media, show up and shake hands and press flesh and sign books. It's fun, though! A lot of people are shy, but I'm not.

How do you feel about being in the public eye all the time?

I would say that most people don't know that I really love being alone. Because when I'm on stage, I'm gregarious, and I want to be with all those people. I hug everybody, I take pictures. For example, we're in China, and I've got 12,000 people who take 14,000 pictures in the next couple of hours and your eyes want to fall out of your head, and you're really ready to get out of it. You finally say, "Enough is enough." Because it takes a lot of energy, whether it's 100 people or 500, and if it's a smaller group, you're going to get hit with everybody's emotion. For example, someone might say, "I read this story when Daddy died! I didn't know I was going to make it without your book." And you're like, "Oh God …"

Yes, it's easy to be affected by other people's emotions if you're a caring person. Tell me about your charitable work. You give a lot, don't you? You like helping and doing charity work.

Well, I ask every author to figure out the end result before they start a book. But then, let's go one step further and say, "*What* are you going to give your money to?" I've written money books, like *One Minute*

Millionaire: you've got to give 10 per cent, invest 10 per cent and save 10 per cent. If you live on 70 per cent of your income, you'll make yourself wealthy *and* source the world like you're supposed to.

So every one of the books I've written has a 10 per cent tithe to it. Now, you may wonder how that works. Well, I wrote a book called *The Miracle of Tithing* – we've tithed every one of the books we've ever done. If you take care of the spiritual stuff, the book sales will take care of themselves, and you'll meet the right people and get the right results.

I've had to drag a lot of people – I won't name them – into giving, because they go, "Oh, I'm not giving. If I give 10 per cent, I'll have less." It's like water. Ice is water that is frozen. That's somebody who doesn't give, right? You're stuck. You're not going to get anything because you're not giving anything. Water, warm, moves. It undulates. Water thawed is vapor: this is what happens when you tithe. One drop of water in your bathroom steams the whole mirror. That's what giving is. Water vaporizes, so you don't have 10 per cent less and end up with 90 per cent. You have 10 per cent that turns into 1,000 per cent and 1 million per cent.

It's a different point of view than anyone else thinks, but then most of my views are a little unusual. I think that's why people read me. They go, "I don't know if I agree with Mark, but boy, he sure pushes my envelope. I'm supposed to think bigger?" You know, it's like when I started, and I told my friend Bob Proctor, "I'm going to sell 50 million and 1000 million and a 500 million and a billion books." Now, he says, "You know, I never want to tell people they can't do it, but boy, when you told me that 20 years ago, I didn't believe you. But now you're a half-billion sold, so I guess you can do it."

So I've got my publishers believing I'm going to sell 10 million copies of *The Miracles in You*, and as a result, they've thought bigger, and they're doing some stuff that nobody would ever do. They're saying, "We're going to be worthy of this. We're going to help you sell 10 million." They didn't believe that you could come out of the chutes and sell 10 million. I said, "Just because it hasn't been done, doesn't mean we can't do it before the end of the year. Let's push. We'll see if we can pull it."

Summary for Super-Busy Entrepreneurs

- Test out your book ideas on your target readers. Get a broad spectrum of feedback, not just from your spouse and editor.

- Ask them to grade your chapters on a scale of one to ten. Parts of your book that are so memorable they want to retell them should be graded as ten-plus-plus-plus!

- For every 1,000 ideas or stories your contributors give, your book may benefit from being distilled down to the best 250.

- Bear in mind that many parts of your book that you love may not "make it" with your readers.

- Welcome feedback. Don't be critical of yourself or the person giving it.

- If you're already well known, blind-test your book and remove your name.

- We are emotional beings. Ensure that your book hits your reader emotionally. Look for stories that give you goosebumps or a tear in the eye.

- If you find a book formula that works, consider doing sequels and prequels. Explore how deep the need is.

- Figure out your end result first. Decide who your market is. Write the book that your market needs rather than the one you want to write.

- If you're approaching publishers, make yourself rejection-proof. When somebody rejects you, just say, "Next!"

- You can still make money from a book without selling millions of copies. Run seminars, teleseminars and coaching alongside your book

- A book gives your business mega-credibility and authority with clients and customers, especially if you sign it.
- Where there is a problem, there is a solution. The knowledge can be written up and shared in a book.
- Build relationship capital – ask colleagues and friends to send out emails to help you with your book launch.
- Promote your book with imaginative videos on YouTube, Google+, Facebook, or any other social media.
- Think of alternative and surrogate ways to promote your book. For example, in car showrooms.
- Write a list of 200 people you'd like to spend time with to make things happen for marketing your book.
- Speaking will sell books but won't necessarily sell enough to achieve bestseller status. Social and electronic media have a wider reach.
- Prepare for media interviews beforehand and have sound bites ready that promote your book. Get someone to grill and test you beforehand.
- Consider tithing your book. Giving away 10% of your profits will have a bigger impact than you think.
- Set yourself big goals, even if they seem unattainable. It will encourage other people like your publishers to think bigger too.

SIMON WOODROFFE, OBE

"I didn't want to write a full-on book because I left school at 16, and I wasn't well educated…"

Simon Woodroffe, OBE, left college aged 16 with two O Levels. He spent 30 years in the entertainment industry before launching a conveyor-belt sushi bar in London.

The concept was to make eating out an entertainment experience with call buttons, robot drinks trolleys, and Japanese TV. The first YO! Sushi restaurant was a phenomenon when it opened, and the business now has more than 70 branches in the UK and overseas.

Simon has appeared as a panellist in the first series of the BBC hit show *Dragons' Den,* as well as numerous other TV shows. He's author of *The Book of YO!* (1ˢᵗ edition, 2000. 2ⁿᵈ edition, 2004).

I'm really proud of *The Book of YO!* I can actually read it myself comfortably 10 years on. So I'm really pleased with it. My inspiration was that I wanted to write a book of some sort. Soon after I started YO! Sushi, I realised that the way to get publicity for the brand and for everything I wanted to do in the future – the way to get a high profile – was not to talk about how good the food was or how nice the restaurant was. That's just not interesting to anybody. So instead, when I started doing press interviews and speeches, I always talked about the world and life and everything according to me. So I thought I'd write a book about the world and life and everything according to me, which was halfway between the acceptable side of personal development and a "how do you do it?" sort of book.

I didn't want to write a full-on book because I left school at 16 and I wasn't well educated, so I find it very hard to read long books. In fact, I wish people would just precis non-fiction so that I could just read a couple of pages and know what it was about. So I thought I'd write one of those. But you know, being a bit of a control freak at the time, especially, I did kind of take it over and decide how I'd like it to be. That's the only thing I regret is that it's slightly "pamphlety". But I am pleased with it, and a lot of people do like it, though some don't get it at all. It's an easy book to dip in and out of, and it sort of tells my story without writing an autobiography.

As you say, a lot of entrepreneurs do choose to write a "how to" book or an autobiography. However, you chose this format because you like information that's short and sweet and condensed down. What sort of responses did you get from your readers?

Well, it's always difficult as the author because most of the people who I talked to said they really loved it. But then people don't like to tell you things that you don't want to hear! But I've always had very, very good responses to it, and people say it's a great book to dip in and out of. Rebecca Stephens, the first woman to climb Everest, who's a friend of mine, has written quite a lot of books. She said to me at dinner one night, "How are you getting on with your book?" I replied, "I finished it." She asked, "How long did it take you?" I said, "Three months." She said, "You're a genius. You're genius." By the time we got to pudding, she said, "How many words is it?" And I said, "About five or six thousand." She said, "That's not a book, that's a fucking pamphlet."

Well, she was to the point! Now, your book is unconventional in many ways. It's 17 cm by 17 cm, so it's square. It's bright orange. A lot of the colours inside are very bright, with lots of photos and images. Was that a deliberate decision from the very outset, or was that just kind of how it turned out?

It was my decision – I wanted to do something different and innovative for people. When I look back on it, it probably wasn't the right way to go, if you want to get a really mainstream book. It was too far ahead of its time. But you know, that's what I did, and I've used it for speeches, and we've printed 35,000 copies now. So we have sold about 30,000 of those. So one way or another, it's done pretty well for a little book like that.

It was me sort of saying, "I know better than you publishers." I think about 10 years ago that was me, and now if I did another book, I wouldn't do that. I never thought it was very well marketed, that book, either. But probably that was because I told everybody what to do and then went on to something else.

In those days, you didn't self-publish. There was no choice. The publisher approached me anyways to write a book. So I said, "Yep. Okay, will do." It all happened in a very short period of time: about six months from idea to publishing.

So tell me about your process for writing your book.

All I did was I said, "I'm going to write this myself; therefore, it's got to be simple. It can't be too complicated as I don't have much time. It's got to be a formula book." The formula was: double-page spread with a headline that captures you at the top of the page. Left-hand side of the page: a story about my life. Right-hand page: what I learned and bullet points, with a photograph to illustrate. Then I wrote down titles of things that I used in my speeches.

Most of it was what they now call being a motivational speaker, which is just me talking about the world and life and everything according to me. I'd got really successful on that speaking circuit. At one time, I was doing one or two a week, and they were paying me really good money as well. So I really got into that, and I thought, "I'll just write a book about what I talk about in my speeches." So I wrote down a lot of those lines such as:

"Wherever you are is where you need to be," or "Spend 90% of your time doing what you love doing." These were all the things that I'd been using in my speeches, then I just expanded on them from my life experience with bullet points. It just was very to the point.

I talked a lot about fear. I talked about the sort of stuff that people used to say to me at the speeches. People would always say, "What's great about you is you're an ordinary bloke like us, so we know ordinary people can do things." And also, "You don't embellish it; you tell it how it was for you and what went on inside you. We can relate to that, and we like it because of that." It was an honest book.

It's still a bestseller on Amazon when I last looked. Did you have a bestseller campaign, or do anything actively to turn your book into a bestseller?

Not really. In fact, I asked Nick [in charge of YO! publicity and promotion] the other day, "Can you still buy it on Amazon?" So, in fact, one of the things on his list is to get it back on Amazon. We'd never really done anything. So it should really be revamped and redone. You remember how you used to have "know-how" books in the old days? I had this idea that I was going to start a publishing company called YO! How. I've never really gotten around to it. That was supposed to be the first book in the YO! How series. That was my idea.

Great idea. So can you share why you decided to have three different editions of your book? People might assume that you write a book and then just leave it. Why did you update it?

Each one hasn't changed very much. But each time we have reprinted it, I've been asked, "Do you want to make any changes?" So I've said, "Yeah, let's put a new photo on and have new intro at the beginning. Let me change a couple of bits in it." I didn't change very much. Just a newer photograph and a new introduction and ending.

A lot of publishers and authors are very happy if they sell 3,000 books. So 35,000 copies is quite an achievement. How have you managed to keep selling those without running a marketing campaign?

I was constantly onto the publisher saying, "Why aren't you doing this? You should be doing that." You know, I was trying to tell them how to do their job, and I think in the end they kind of got fed up with it really. They gave me the rights back, and I never really followed it up because by that time I was on to something else. So you know, if I launch another book, I think I'd probably re-launch *The Book of YO!* as well.

Great! So let's look at another aspect of your book. The blurb is often one of the things authors use for search engine optimisation on Amazon. But you don't have a blurb on your book covers. Instead, you've got lots of endorsements and quotes from the media. Why did you make that decision?

Well, first of all, I wasn't aware of what you just said. So I just suggested to the designer that's what they do, and they went along with this. The publisher maybe wasn't strong enough at the time to say, "No, we want to do it this way. We want to do that," which is what a publisher should do. They should stand up to the author, and say, "No, you should do this."

So, mine's a very good example of somebody in a reasonably powerful position who said, "Look, I know better than you guys how to do it." In some ways, it worked for me, and I produced exactly what I wanted. In other ways, it didn't work because it hasn't been constantly marketed over the years, and eventually, the publisher dropped it because I was a difficult author. There's a lesson to learn out of that!

As you mentioned earlier, you left school at 16 with two O levels. Did you feel nervous about writing a book and exposing things in your personal life – the successes and the failures?

No, I didn't. I suppose we all have a face and a façade that we put on. I call it a mask. On the one hand, I am a bit of an actor, and I've always hidden behind the mask. But part of that has been really exposing myself and making myself quite vulnerable. I heard an expression, "Vulnerability with dignity," once. I think it was Mick Jagger of all people who said it. Vulnerability with dignity is a very, very attractive trait. So I've always tried to do that and to be very open and honest about my failures and my character defects. I find that is something that people can relate to and that they like in a human being, rather than being too slick and putting your best face on the whole time. Just be fairly honest. As we go through life, we all have our ways of doing things, and that works quite well for me. So no, I'm not scared.

Underneath it, I do have fear like everybody. But when I feel like I'm in the groove, which I did when I was writing that book because I've had five years of doing speeches and people clapping loudly at the end of them, I had a certain confidence that what I was saying was right and would resonate and people would like it. I was pretty confident of that. Then of course, soon after that book came out, I did the Edinburgh Festival as a stand-up comic effectively, with a show called, "How I got my YO!".

Having written the book and done the corporate speeches, I thought it was going to be a major hit at the Edinburgh Festival. Though I got away with it, and we did have audiences, and I got good reviews for the most part, although I also got "Worst of the Festival" from somebody and had a real shock because I wasn't the kind of star of the show which I'd hoped I would be. It was a real struggle. I did 23 shows in a row, and I really struggled to go into houses that weren't full always. That really brought me down to earth. There was quite a big difference between corporate speeches and going on to be entertainment. So you get your ups and your downs, and that was a humbling experience. You can't just take one thing and translate it into another always.

Would you say it's possible to make money from a book without selling millions of copies?

I would have thought you could these days. Just as a businessman adding it up on the back of my fag packet as I talk to you, I would think that if you self-publish and make all the margin, it's not very expensive to print a book, as I found out having printed a couple of editions myself. Distribution is only putting something in the back of your car, or selling it at speeches, or putting it on an Internet site. People do buy them, and you make all the margin yourself. So I'm sure that you can make money this way.

If I do a book again, I don't really want to do a book unless it has the potential to have quite the big impact and be a bit of a bestseller and something that people talk about.

I remember Julian Richer telling me at the time he had written *Richer Sounds* (which is quite a successful book) that he knew getting on the WH Smith list was probably the best way to sell books, as they sold more than anybody else. All the publishers were saying this, that and the other. So he just phoned up the buyer at WH Smith, and said, "Oh, my name is Julian Richer, can I come and see you? I'm an author." And the guy said, "Oh, I've bought a stereo in one of your shops. And authors never, ever call me. Come on over."

So he went over. He said, "Look, this is what I've done. Have a look at the book." The guy said, "Oh, that sounds good. Just let us know when, and we'll put it on the list." And Julian said, "Okay." So he just got his secretary to pack them up and send them off to WH Smith every couple of months. You know, kind of simple. Same as Miles Copeland when The Police started. He couldn't get the right record company deal, so he bought a blue transit van, got the records pressed, put them all in the back of the van and drove them out around the country himself and put them in the record stores. The guy said, "Push these, will you mate?" and it worked. And The Police got a very good record deal, eventually.

Yes, a lot of these ideas are simple but very effective. It was a similar story when James Redfield travelled around book stores in America giving away free copies of *The Celestine Prophecy*...

Earlier, we talked about the quotes on the back of your book. Let's talk media now. Many entrepreneurs will want to know what you did to get those quotes...

Those are all quotes from speeches I've done. In fact, if you look on the back of the book, there's one from somebody called David Twiggy

Molecey. Anyways, I did a speech at the Institute of Directors once, and as I was coming out, I overheard this guy on the other side of the corridor saying, "That was the best speech I've heard at the Institute of Directors in 10 years."

So I turned to the bloke next to me. I said, "Who's that bloke?" He said, "He's called David Twiggy Molecey." I wrote it down in my notebook. That was his name, and I heard him say it, so I put it on the back of the book.

What about the quotes from the newspapers?

That's just stuff that I collected. I always was a real believer in what I call third party endorsements, or what I call "desired customer response". When you tell people how good your thing is going to be, whatever it is – your book, business, or whatever – most people go, "Yeah, yeah. I've heard it all before." But if *somebody else* says, "It's great," you listen.

So if one person says to me, "Stephanie Hale is just such a brilliant book marketer," there's one sentence that I hear, and that goes in. That registers. When I hear it from a second person or a third person, I'm seriously interested. Whereas if you tell me how great you are, I'm not really going to listen.

I won't try telling you how great I am then! So can you share some of your tips for being interviewed by the media? You've done numerous interviews in your time with newspapers, radio, television – whereas many entrepreneurs are a bit wary of journalists. What sort of things can you do to ensure that you give a good interview?

Well, when I did *Question Time*, I went to the green room before the show, and I said to David Dimbleby, "Look, I've not done this before. Quite an imposing show. Give me some advice." He said, "Do you know in all my years of doing this, nobody's ever asked me that question? So I will. Number one, don't have a point of view so much as talk about what *your experience* is and how this topic relates to *you* as a businessman and what's happened. So talk from yourself. Number two, talk directly to the audience. And number three, remember when you're not talking, the camera could still be on you." At that point, he held his finger up to his nose.

So the first one I think is absolutely right. What I've always done is to talk about what my experience is in the world, rather than what you should do, or they should do. It's amazing because no one can criticise that if you talk about what your feeling is. I was talking about exactly this on Bloomberg the day before yesterday. I did a long interview with them about it. What I said was, "Look, on most of these political issues, I could argue both sides of the argument. Yet most people who sit in this seat, doing an interview with you here on Bloomberg, have one adamant point of view which they push. Whereas actually, I can argue both sides of most of those things. And often, whichever one you decide, you can change later. Doesn't make a great deal of difference, but the important thing is to decide and move on." So that's what I think.

Let's discuss the impact of being a personality and how it feels to go out and have people recognise you in the street. Do you feel this is a positive or a negative thing? Or do you have mixed feelings?

I actually like it. I remember when I did the first series of *Dragon's Den*. You know, we had a lot of good press about it immediately and a very good reaction from viewers. People would recognise us in the street. I phoned everybody else up to see what they thought, and they all had their point of view. I phoned Duncan Bannatyne up, and I said, "What do you think, Duncan?" He actually said these words – you can tone them down if you like – he said, "People recognise me on the street, Simon. I fucking love it!" I'm quite gregarious, and I do like all of that to tell you the truth. I very much like being recognised. I like being able to be the ordinary bloke on the street, and I always engage in conversations as an equal and I'm interested in other people.

Tell me a little about the highs and lows in your journey. It's easy to look at a successful person and assume, "Oh, it's alright for him, he's been on *Dragon's Den*, and he's a well-known author."

Well, it's always been a struggle really; my whole life business-wise has been a struggle. I was a roadie first, and then I went on tour with bands, and there was always the competition to see whether I could get on this tour or that tour and get the job. Then I wanted to move up and do the lighting, and then I was a small company doing designs for stage sets. I was always trying to compete with other people to get the job and to get the right price. There were lots of knockbacks. The music business was pretty unscrupulous in those days, and being ripped off along the way. Then I was in the television business, selling television rights, and some of the deals worked, and some of them didn't.

So there's always been lots of ups and downs and failures. What I've realised over the years is that the greatest assets that I've got are enthusiasm and ignorance because I cannot think too much, and I don't mind being rejected. I don't like it, nor does anybody, and I love acclaim. But I am willing to go out and take a risk and stand up and have people poo-poo me. But if you do it with enough confidence, believe it or not, people think, "Oh my God, he might have something!"

Then when we launched YO! Sushi, the first week it was empty, and the second week we had a queue down the block. So there you go: that first week I had everything sunk into it, and it could all have gone terribly wrong. And we opened second and third restaurants at Selfridges and Harvey Nichols, and one on Finchley Road, and they were all going swimmingly.

Then we opened County Hall and one in Edinburgh, and they went really badly. Suddenly, we had two haemorrhaging and four pulling in money. So from being this hottest thing on the block, we were in trouble. Then we had the floor break up at Poland Street, the first one, and I didn't have enough money to repair it. As I always used to say in those days: the money was rolling in, and the money was rolling right back out again.

I would say over the first five years until Sir Robin Rowland joined, and even after that actually until we made our first sale when I reduced my shareholding, there were at least three times when we were very close to the edge and we could have gone bankrupt. I always said there was once when I had to roll a four on the dice, and a couple of times I had to roll a two or three or more. So there were times it definitely could have gone wrong. The whole thing! I wouldn't be sitting here on the phone with you today: I don't know what I would have done. Maybe I would have stopped, started again, and built something else up. But there were definitely some moments.

Then we had the YO! Below Bars, which I thought were very good, but eventually, we closed. We had YO! Japan, the clothing range. We had the YO! How publishing, which never really took off. We had RadiYO! which never really took off. There's been lots of things that haven't worked along the way, and the two things that have worked are YO! Sushi, and YOTEL. Now we're putting ourselves on the line again with YO! Home.

So it has not all been success by a long shot, though from the outside it always looks like that. Definitely, I have had failures. Though it's better now because for a long time, for much of my life, failure to me meant I might not be able to eat, and I might lose everything that I'd got. Now it doesn't mean that. It means I've got to put a bit more into it. Or it doesn't feel very good to say, "Oh, I won't do that." But it doesn't mean that I'm going to be out of my house and home. So this is a very good place to be. It's a high-class problem. People who've made money will tell you that the worry at our age is that you'll lose it for the rest of your life and your family. But, as I say, it's a high-class problem, and one I'm happy to have. Although I've taken lots of risks in my life, and I like to have some of my money at risk, I'm pretty conservative in many ways.

You've got an idea for another book at the moment, haven't you? Tell me a little more about this.

I read *Outliers* by Malcolm Gladwell and was very taken with the idea of it. So I came up with the title of, *What Made Me Me.* I was going to take 30 instances that have happened in my life, and how they affected me. You'd read it as a way of seeing what made me, me. But it would also make you think about what made you, you.

Now when I was a kid growing up, I always used to think that if you told people your ideas, they'd steal them. Generally, in this world, my experience has been that this doesn't happen – that much more traction is created by talking about your ideas, and it also talks you out of impotence and into getting them done! So I've always talked about my ideas. So I've told quite a few people including you that I've got an idea for a new book called *What Made Me Me*. If somebody nicks my idea, I'll just think of something else to do!

I've written one book; I'd like to do another one. I've done lots of things in my life. I've done speeches and been on television. I've made a record with The Blockheads called *How I Got My YO!* which I'm pretty proud of. I've been in the restaurant business. I'm in the property business. I've been in the hotel business. I've done a bit of publishing. There's a kind of realisation that anybody can do anything: it's like The American Dream. So I'm always keen to try out new things. I wrote a book, and it was successful, and I was pleased with it. So I think I'm rather remiss in not having written another one to follow it up. At some point, I'd like to do that.

Summary for Super-Busy Entrepreneurs

- Talking about how great your service or product is won't be interesting to your readers. A better approach is to write about the world and life and everything according to you.

- You don't have to write a lengthy tome. You can still get your message across in a shorter book that readers can dip in and out of.

- You don't have to write a conventional book. Consider writing something innovative with bright-coloured pages and images, or with an unconventional size or layout.

- If you're a speaker, use topics from your talks and expand upon them. Think about feedback from your audience and use this to guide you when thinking about the contents and tone of your book.

- If you get your books reprinted, use this as an opportunity to revise and update your content. Freshen up your introduction and ending, and even your front cover.

- When other people praise your work, it carries a great deal more weight. Quotes and endorsements have a much bigger impact.

- People relate better to vulnerability than to putting on your best face all the time. Be honest about your failures and character defects.

- Take responsibility for your own book marketing. This may mean calling WH Smith yourself or giving away sample copies of your book. Simple forms of marketing can often be very effective.

- For media interviews, talk about what *your experience* is and how a topic relates to *you* rather than taking a standpoint. Talk directly to your audience, and remember that the camera could still be on you even when you're not talking.

- Be willing to take risks and have people poo-poo you. If you do things with enough confidence, they'll think, "Oh my God, s/he might have something!"

- Sharing your book idea with others talks you out of impotence and into getting it done. Other people are very unlikely to steal your ideas.

KELLY HOPPEN, MBE

"Writing a book with dyslexia is very challenging..."

Kelly Hoppen, MBE, is a graphic designer who counts many of the world's elite – including David and Victoria Beckham – as her clients.

Kelly started her career at the age of 16 when she was given the opportunity to design a kitchen for a family friend. This modest commission kick-started an award-winning career in the design industry.

She went on to become founder of Kelly Hoppen Interiors and is author of 10 design books. She is known for her subtle East meets West fusion and has put her stamp on homes, yachts, and jets for private clients all over the world. She now focuses on commercial projects including hotels, restaurants, and tower blocks.

Her TV and film appearances include a cameo role in the *Absolutely Fabulous* movie alongside Joanna Lumley and Jennifer Saunders, as well as being an investor in BBC 2's hit show Dragons' Den. She's also fronted the Channel 5 design series, Superior Interiors.

My books come from the designs I have always produced and the houses that I transform. What my aim was, and is, is to put my intricate designs combining western and eastern cultures together in book form. I wanted to share my knowledge with people and inspire them to achieve the home of their dreams.

Please share a little about your writing process. Was it easy to transfer your creative principles from interior design over to writing?

Having dyslexia will always make such a project challenging, but I overcame such hardship with the amazing help from my publishers. Already having the creative elements allowed me to envision the final outcome. As for the writing process, I worked with some amazing writers who helped extract all the information from my brain, and together we expressed exactly what I wanted to achieve.

You're dyslexic, as are a great many celebrities that I work with. Was this an "issue" for you when you first started writing your books?

Writing a book with dyslexia is very challenging as I am very thorough and wanted to ensure it was all perfect. I have learnt to work with my dyslexia; I don't see it as a problem any more.

Your book *East Meets West* is credited with "making you famous". Tell me more about this and what happened.

I was very inspired by my travels around Asia and Europe, and I wanted to put together designs that would incorporate elements from different cultures. This was something quite different to be published, and my aim was to simply put my already-developing ideas into a book that could be shared. I have been in the design industry for almost 40 years now, and my design work and style is what I like to think got me to where I am today; it was what I started with, my foundation for everything else I've done.

What sort of an impact has each of your books had on your business?

The books document my work, my techniques, and my style, which I wanted to share. The use of my business is design, and the books and products are a great addition to the brand I created.

Did your books help you in getting on TV and getting media attention in the early days?

Not really with TV, but yes with media, as every time I launch a book the media want to see and write about it.

Your books are mostly sold as high-end hardback, with a price point around £24. Was this a deliberate decision not to go mass market with a paperback?

Paperbacks cannot be preserved as well as hardback books, and I want people to be satisfied with what they buy. To me, the look and feel of a book is as important as its content. I also really enjoy the feel of coffee table books; I think they can add a beautiful personal touch to your rooms, and they are also great sources for conversation starters. My current publisher Jacqui Small is great at publishing hardback books.

How do you go about choosing your title or cover designs?

For the cover design, it's simply a picture that truly sums up the style of that particular book. I have the critical eye to make sure the image is the absolute perfect one. It is very important to choose an image that will attract the audience. The title usually comes easily to me; sometimes I come up with it first, and the book content follows.

You've worked with co-authors for a couple of your books. How do you choose the right person and ensure a harmonious working relationship?

I meet with the writers and make sure they fully understand me and what my style is all about.

Do you do anything to market your books? If so, what?

Normally, we have a PR campaign. The publishers work on marketing, but this is minimal as there is so much demand for the books.

Do you ever feel anxious pre-launch about how your books will be received?

No one can ever be sure of how something is going to be received by others; I just focus on the great content and knowledge I'm sharing.

What have been your best (and worst) moments while writing your books?

Seeing the final proof is amazing! There is no worst moment.

Do you have plans to write more books?

Yes, I am always coming up with new ideas and would love to share them. Also, my fortieth year in the business is coming up, and I am in the process of writing a retrospective book on my career so far.

What sort of books do you enjoy reading yourself?

I enjoy non-fiction books about business, design, and fashion. I really enjoy Deepak Chopra's books, as he is an inspiration with great lessons to teach.

Summary For Super-Busy Entrepreneurs

- Illustrations and pictures can be an important part of your book, especially if this ties in with your business. Inspiration can come from your own visual designs, style, and physical creations.
- Share your knowledge to inspire others and help them achieve their dreams.
- Writing a book with dyslexia can be a challenge, but it doesn't have to be a problem.
- Your book can document your work, your techniques, and your style so that you share them with potential clients and customers.
- Your books should be a great addition to your business brand.
- Books can help you with getting attention from journalists. The media is likely to be especially interested at the time of your book launch.
- Think about the look and feel of a book as well as its content.
- A hardback book will have greater longevity and be more durable than a paperback.
- If you co-author a book, make sure you meet with the writers first to make sure they fully understand you and your style.
- Coffee table books add a beautiful personal touch to rooms and are great conversation starters. They are more likely to stay lying around.
- It's essential to choose an image for your book cover that will attract your target audience.

GARY RHODES, OBE

"I want my cookery books to look tatty around the edges
... because readers don't want to stop using them"

Restaurateur and TV chef, Gary Rhodes, OBE, is well known for his love of British cuisine and has won a constellation of Michelin stars.

He has cooked for royalty, prime ministers, and presidents throughout his 35-year career and currently runs many restaurants in Dubai and the Caribbean.

He's had a successful television career, fronting shows including: *MasterChef, Hell's Kitchen, Rhodes Around Britain,* and *The Great British Food Revival.* He was also a contestant in *Strictly Come Dancing.*

He's been prolific as a writer and is author of over 20 books.

Rhodes Around Britain tells the story about the great old British classics. I wrote it in 1993, and it was published in 1994. In 1999, *New British Classics* came out and was probably my biggest book and the one that took the absolute longest of the lot to write. But with that book, my whole style with British food had developed. I think it took it to another level.

During those five years, I had one book a year being published. It was a continual learning process, and an education for me, and I wanted to share that learning with the general public. I think sometimes those books were a bit long-winded. When I look back, compared with the way I write today, I probably gave too much detail. Quite often, the introduction to the recipes – particularly in *New British Classics* – was even longer than the recipe itself! That was because I wanted to tell the history of the dish. I wanted to talk about its origins, how it was developed, and what I'd done to it rather than just giving the reader an '*A, B, C, stir, simmer for five minutes*' sort of scenario.

I think I wanted to remind everyone of what this country had stood for on the culinary scene, as well as how it could be refined and shown off at its best.

Do you feel that by writing your books, it's helped to separate you from other chefs by stamping some of your personality on them?

Obviously, it helps to tell a story. It establishes what my culinary personality is all about. But sometimes I feel it has worked against me, in that people think that's all I know or all I do. And that is not me at all.

I was trained in French cuisine and, over the years, I've worked in endless different countries and still do lots of culinary events all over the world.

In fact, I'm in Malaysia in a couple of weeks' time, and I'll be promoting British cuisine. Even when I was in Tokyo and Saigon last year, all I wanted to show off was British cooking. But while I'm in these amazing countries, I make sure that in any spare time I happen to have I'm eating out so I get to see what the local food and dishes are all about. That's what I thrive on: looking, learning, and tasting. That's what I enjoy so much about this career. People say to me, "When are you going to retire?" Retire? I don't want to retire. I never want to retire.

There was a quote I once read which pretty much sums up my philosophy. A few years ago, I had flown to South Africa to take over a restaurant for a few weeks and, as I arrived in Cape Town, I saw this huge quote on the airport wall which said, 'The road to success is always under construction.' That has stuck in my mind, and I try and tutor it to all my team here: that a career in this industry is a continual education. You can never stop and think, "Okay, I've done it now. Great. I can give up." Because all the while I can come back with another little idea, with another something to spark me off, and I'm thinking – I get almost annoyed – why didn't I think of that? But, you know, at the same time I thrive on it and want to use it and take that tip or hint to increase the quality of what I'm already creating.

When I'm talking about food, I can become obsessive about it, and I sometimes think I must be boring the pants off everyone because it's what I love talking about the most. I also love talking about restaurants, the whole great social event of it all. One of the most important things to me is the dinner table at home. It's that family service when all of you are together, enjoying each other's company and enjoying what you're eating, with simple food. I don't cook Michelin-starred restaurant food at home.

I'll do a roast leg of lamb with all the trimmings like everyone else. But it's just enjoying what you've done and taking that little extra care with it.

You obviously like pushing yourself to your limits. You mention writing a book per year at one point. How do you find the time?

When I wrote *Rhodes Around Britain,* it took me well over a year. At the time, I was actually employed by somebody else, so I had a job to do as well. It was written on my days off or in my spare time, so it took some time. Did I really know how to write a book back then? I suppose I learnt as I went along.

It was the same with *New British Classics* all those years later; that took over a year because there was so much research involved. I had somebody researching things for me, but I had to put it all together: what I wanted researched, what I wanted done, and then I would take the information they gave me, break it down, put my own take on it, and make sure it was coming from me. But I had to do it like that, otherwise I would never have got through writing that book.

But I suppose today, it's very different. Now, I don't include those long, long introductions because I think the audience has changed. I think there was a time when people found it entertaining to read a story about where a dish was born, and what I'd done to it to give you the recipe that was sitting underneath. But it's changed, and I think nowadays it's more about simplicity and speed. You don't want to spend a lifetime reading a book, and you certainly don't want to see a recipe that goes on for a page-and-a-half.

I think people now want a three-line introduction – *this dish is made from whatever, or you can supplement it with such and such if it's unavailable* –

that kind of scenario. Then, underneath, you have no more than six to eight ingredients, and you'll find two of them are salt and pepper and one of them is a squeeze of lemon or knob of butter. So keep it simple. You've got a method which is no more than five categories: prep, cook, finish, here's how you serve it, with a nice picture to go with it.

Obviously, when you have a book deal you're given a deadline, and you're told when it has to be published by, and so forth, and you have to keep to that. Quite often, you'll get a minimum of eight months to a year. Once, I was so busy with work that I got to one month before the deadline and I still hadn't written a word! Having said that, I still got the book written and to the publisher on time, but that's because I had one month of me saying, "I'm out of bounds. Don't anyone harass me." It helps that these days I'm my own boss, so I can say, "Right, that's it! I'm running late." Sometimes I'd go into work and sit in my office and write recipes all day, and other times I found it easier to stay at home and would literally only stop for supper. Then, I'd continue writing until one or two o'clock in the morning, get a few hours' sleep, and then come back down and continue. Would I choose to do that again? No, I wouldn't.

But things have changed over the years. Nowadays, big heavy cookery books often become big heavy coffee table books. I want my cookery books to look tatty around the edges after six months because the readers don't want to stop using them. So, instead of me writing a book about my restaurant dishes – which then people won't use because the recipes are too complicated – I want to show them what sort of food I like to eat at home, keeping it really simple and trying to make sure that nothing is too expensive so that it's accessible to everyone. I'll also say, '*If you are not a great lover of whatever or you don't eat shellfish, why don't you replace it with…'* giving hints and tips along the way. What I'm trying to say is "Look. Don't be over-led by this book. These are guidelines. I'm trying to give you some ideas that might spark off other ideas of your own." I still love writing cookery books, but I love it because, again, it makes me work that little bit harder in creating dishes for them – and for me.

How do you keep coming up with fresh ideas?

That's a good question. I suppose it's because not only do I write cookery books, I collect them. It drives my wife absolutely insane, and now when I buy one I have to hide it. I've got over 2,500 cookery books, though I know people who have got infinitely more. I think it's Anton Mosimann, who is a legend of a man and a chef, who has collected something like 10,000 cookery books, so I'm nowhere near him. But all the same, it's an awful lot of cookery books. Sometimes, just reading something very small or just taking one idea from a book might spark off another idea, which helps you actually create dishes. I love that. You're not taking that idea, just an element of it; I don't want to copy other people.

My favourite pastime in the world is eating out. You're looking at the whole restaurant itself, not just the food. *What is actually happening? What's the mood of everybody today? What's the style of that restaurant?* Now today, of course, it's all about sharing plates on the table, four or five dishes, everyone scoffs away and helps themselves. It is a lot more relaxed than it used to be. Even the dress code of people at restaurants has changed over the years. I take all this in because that can often tell you the mood of the food. So I always stick by what I believe in, but I try to ensure that if I need to mould it slightly to suit the general public, then that's what I'll do.

You made your first TV appearance at age 27. Tell me a little about the transition between being a chef in the kitchen to being on national television.

Yes, that was a very interesting time. I'd been at The Castle Hotel in Taunton for one year at that stage. There was a chap that used to do breakfast television called Glynn Christian, and he was one of the few cooks on Breakfast TV. He had his own cookery school just off Tottenham Court Road in London, and he wanted to get a Michelin-starred chef to do a cookery demo at his school. He contacted me and said, "Look, I've read about you recently. Would you be willing to come up to London? Would you like to come and do a cookery demo?" I'd never done a cookery demo before in my life, but I said, "Okay, yeah." He told me, "I want you to do some of the British classics you're doing at the moment at the restaurant." So that was no problem, and I went along.

It was only when I got there he told me, "By the way, the people here are working for a large company, and there's 30 different chefs coming." Then, I thought, 'Oh my God! I'm doing a cooking demo to 30 chefs.' But I went on, and from what I can remember, I was very quiet to begin with: "Erm, welcome. I'm delighted you're all here today." And it was all a bit stagnant and quiet. Then it suddenly came to me: *What are you doing? Just talk to them the way you talk to your own cooks in your kitchen. Talk to them the way you talk to a guest eating in the restaurant.*

So then I switched gear and said, "Guess what? Now I'm going to excite you about this food because these are great British classics. I'm going to show you a different edge, a different detail of how you can take these on to another level." So, I did the demo, and afterwards Glynn Christian said to me, "You know, you could have a future in television here. I've videoed it, and I'm going to speak to a TV company." I said "Thanks very much, that's very kind," and off I went, thinking, 'Yeah, sure. He's just being kind and nice.'

There weren't many chefs on TV at that time. We'd all had galloping Graham Kerr back in the early 70s, we'd had Fanny Craddock from the 50s and 60s, and Delia was also around then. We had Keith Floyd, who was probably the main man at that time. But you didn't really see what I would call 'professional chefs' on TV. Anyway, 48 hours later, I got a phone call from a TV company who were doing something for BSkyB at that time. They said, "Would you consider coming to do five programmes for us? Only a 15-minute slot on each of these programmes, Monday to Friday?" So off I went to do that, which again was in London. Then I had BBC Breakfast TV asking: "Can you come and do a slot here?" The same happened on ITV, and that just went on and on until one day, the BBC said, "We'd like you to come and do your own series." I said, "Oh, is it morning or is it an afternoon?" And they replied, "No. It's eight-thirty in the evening." Then, it dawned on me, "Eight-thirty? Prime time?" I couldn't believe it.

There are some chefs out there, who I'm not going to name, who kind of gave up their career so that they could cook on TV. They still cook away, but they don't own restaurants any more; they're not even the head chef of a restaurant. It's all about being a celeb. I couldn't do that. I don't ever look at myself like that, and never have. Don't get me wrong, there are some great upsides: you get invited to movie premieres; you're there on the big night, outside on the red carpet, and you can get a little bit carried away with it all. But I'm very lucky there, as Jennie – my wife – has always kept my feet firmly on the ground. Jennie will say: "Remember, you're up early tomorrow, and you're going into work." I'll reply, "I know that, darling, I know. But I'm just enjoying this moment." Jennie will remind me: "Enjoy it while you can because tomorrow you're back in that kitchen, chopping this and that." She used to bring me back down to earth every time and still does.

I'm glad I never got carried away with it all. I always recognise and realise my career is my life. Television is that lovely supplement and bonus that goes with it. I still feel very strongly about that today. There's talk about me doing something again on prime time TV. So, it hasn't disappeared, but if it never happened again, would I miss it? Perhaps a bit, but I've got my career anyway, so it's not something I need to do. If they're still interested, then I'm still happy. If not, I'm still happy because I love what I do. So I'll never rely on it.

You find people tend to react to you differently when you've been on TV. In some respects, it can be good for business because you'd get many customers wanting to come to your restaurant hoping they might meet you. I'm not one of these chefs that walk about looking for praise, but if someone says, "Table 12 would like for you to come and say hello," then I'll say, "Sure, no problem – I'll be out there in five minutes." I don't mind that at all. That happened an awful lot. I think I was one of the first professional chefs to get his own prime time TV show with the BBC. Thereafter, of course, we've had an endless number of chefs. So now I feel the public excitement has waned slightly. Nowadays, they don't choose to go to restaurants and expect to see those chefs, but in those days they certainly did.

You've had phenomenal success in lots of different areas, but your journey hasn't always been smooth, has it? Tell me about some of the challenges you had along the way.

My very first challenge was quite a major challenge. When leaving college, all the other chefs wanted to go to London, and I thought, 'I don't want to do that. I want to go abroad, I want to work in France.' I remember writing to some of the greats, the legends: Roger Vergé, Paul Bocuse, Michel Guérard, the Troisgros brothers. All of these great people had three Michelin-starred restaurants, and I've still got the letters from the people who did reply saying, *Thank you, but no thank you, Mr. Rhodes.* In the end, I realised I wasn't going to get into those kinds of restaurants, so I wrote to Hilton Hotels, and I sent them my CV. I wrote to Paris, Amsterdam, Dusseldorf, Brussels, Zurich... The one that came back straight away, or pretty quickly, was the Amsterdam Hilton saying: *We'd like to offer you a job.* So I took it. I remember on the first day of work, they said, "Look. Here's the rota on the wall, so you know exactly when you're working." I suddenly saw that for the next 12 days I was working solidly throughout the whole day, from early in the morning until last thing at night. You'd get an hour off in the afternoon and then be back again for the evening. It was a long, long day. You're doing 12 days in a row like this. I'd never done that before, coming straight from college.

Then, a couple of English guys who worked there said, "Look. You've been in Amsterdam for 12 days, and you haven't even been out and seen anything. You know, things go on until the early hours here. You're off tomorrow. When we've all finished – about eleven-thirty at night – let's go up into town, and we'll find a bar and just have a bit of fun, enjoy it." So we finished, and the three of us were walking from the hotel, and we heard the tram coming to take us to town. We ran to jump on it, and I looked the wrong way, and the next thing I was run over by a Transit van. I was taken to hospital and had to have major surgery. A week later, I was flown back to the UK, in hospital there, and then I ended up being out of work for just under six months.

The kindest thing was that the Amsterdam Hilton saved my job for me, and I went back out there and did another three years. That was one of the most difficult points because I felt a little bit wary of going back there to that place because of the accident. But I'm so pleased I did. I'm so pleased I just got on with it. So, that was not a great start to my career, but from then on, it got an awful lot better.

It's not always been easy, though, and you go through tough times. Even here in Dubai today, it's been a really tough year on everybody, business-wise. Business has been booming for many, many years here, and now it's been hit quite hard. When I opened my first restaurant here nine years ago, there were very few restaurants compared with today. Now, there are 19,000 restaurants in Dubai, but there are not an awful lot more customers. So things have got tighter, but I'm pleased to say we're still open and still successful. So that is a good sign. But you can go through very tough times when you can't afford to keep all of your staff. Then it's about just knuckling down.

It hasn't always been the easiest career, but regardless, I always feel positive about it. I'm positive about all those little mistakes I've made and the fact that I managed to get back on track. You learn from mistakes, you really do. Rather than becoming defeatist, I think, 'So, it didn't go so well there, but at least I know I can cook!'

Do you read your reviews and pay any attention to them?

I do. I've often been told by others, "Don't read it," but over the years, and being a head chef, you're always going to get a review. Particularly once my name was either recognized or known after all the Michelin stars, you'd have write-ups just to keep you ahead on all the places in London. There were some food writers out there who I think just didn't like me. They didn't like me on TV. And there were one or two who had written great things before I was on TV, and then the moment I started doing TV their whole sort of approach changed. I thought my food had improved, but I was getting hammered for it. I found that really depressing, to begin with.

There are great writers out there, such as Jonathan Meades, who I think is the greatest of the lot from *The Times*. He's an absolutely brilliant writer and a wonderful man. That's not just because he wrote great things about me! What I loved was the way he gave his critique; it was something you could learn from and take from, and at the same time, he would pay compliments where he thought the balance of flavours were right. He really talked about the dish, in a way that showed he understood, and you thought, 'That man knows what he's talking about.' You could almost taste the flavours as you were reading what he'd written.

I still do read the reviews, of course I read them, but now I like to take each as a positive regardless of the criticism that may appear. I think the writers that are over here in Dubai aren't quite as brutal as some of the ones in the UK. They will still criticise where it's due, but I always take the positive from it. I stop and think about it, rather than writing it off and throwing it in the bin and thinking, 'How dare they?' I think when you're younger you tend to do that because you don't think you're doing anything wrong.

One of the biggest problems as a chef is that, when you're creating dishes, you make that dish up, and there's half a dozen of you tasting that one little dish. So you're getting not even a tablespoon of it, and you're thinking, 'Oh, that's lovely! Wonderful!' You haven't actually realised the balance of eating that whole dish by yourself. So consequently, strength of flavours can change, and maybe then you're left with a flavour that is overtaking the other. So I look at that in more of a solid way now. When I'm creating dishes, we tutor absolutely everybody – chefs in the kitchen and front of house – to make sure they understand the food. I'll cook several dishes to make sure that everybody has a really damn good taste and understands what the balance is, what the strength is. Does it create perfection? I don't think there's ever such a thing. But if you can get closer to that, then that's a good step. So, now I look at a critique as a positive because then hopefully, I'll learn something from it.

Finally, do you have any plans for any more books?

I'd love to. Rather than always being in the kitchen, it's a great way of expressing yourself. When people come for that one experience, and maybe they've only had a starter, a main course, and dessert, really and truly they don't know the full you. I think the beauty of a book is that you can make every single dish within it approachable, but at the same time give some little bit of magic that will inspire the reader. I won't write about dishes that I feature on the menu today, but I certainly will write about how my approach to eating has changed and create more home-style food with a fresh edge.

Summary For Super-Busy Entrepreneurs

- Writing books is a continual education. Just because a style or format works once doesn't mean it will always be this way.

- You may need to adapt your style and tone when reader expectations change.

- Your book can be used to establish your personality and help you stand out from competitors.

- If time is scarce, consider getting someone else to do all your background research for your book for you.

- If you're using someone to help you, break down the information so it has your personal stamp and voice, and it's coming from you.

- Readers don't like long-winded introductions and instructions these days. They prefer simplicity and speed.

- Book deadlines with publishers are around 8 to 12 months minimum.

- Don't be deceived by a long publishing deadline. If you're busy, you may find you don't start work on your book until a month beforehand.

- You can still get your book written in a month even if you're frantically busy. But you may need to work late and get little sleep.

- Tell friends and family, "I'm out of bounds. Don't anyone harass me," to help you focus and get your book finished.

- Consider if you want your book to become a pristine 'coffee table book' or a book that gets tatty around the edges from people using it.

- Become a prolific reader: buy and read hundreds of books by other experts in your industry.
- Other books might spark off fresh ideas. You're not copying or plagiarising, you're simply using elements of other people's ideas.
- For TV appearances or show-reels, talk in a relaxed, informal way as you would to your staff, a client or a customer.
- Read reviews and take the positives from them, regardless of what is written about you.
- Consider criticism, rather than thinking, 'How dare they?' See if you can learn something from it.
- Your customers may only experience a small percentage of what you can do. The beauty of a book is that it can give them a better idea of the full you.

MARTYN DAWES

"I had to tell the truth about what it's really like."

Martyn Dawes is founder of Coffee Nation, which started with the simple idea to put takeaway coffee in newsagents. He already had a successful management consultancy, but risked everything to start a business with a real product.

Martyn went on to secure contracts with leading retailers such as Tesco, Sainsbury, Esso, Welcome Break and Somerfield. Within 10 years, he had over 600 Coffee Nation kiosks across the UK and had sold over 100 million cups of coffee. He sold his business for £23 million in 2008; it was sold again for £60 million to Whitbread/Costa in 2011.

Martyn is author of "Wake Up and Sell the Coffee", which he wrote to help other people succeed in business. He's been named Entrepreneur of the Year by Ernst & Young and also won the *Sunday Times*/Virgin Atlantic Fast Track Innovation Award. He now mentors CEOs and founders of ambitious growth companies helping them navigate a similar path.

When I was a child, from as long back as I can remember, I knew I was different. I was adopted and I think that gave me the idea that I was always going to be different. I think somehow that propelled me from there. I decided I didn't want to go to university when my peers were all planning where they were going to go. I thought, 'I don't fancy it. I want to get going on my career.' So, I was going against the flow really.

Even in 1996, the word 'entrepreneur' was kind of non-existent in Britain. The first entrepreneur that I really read about was Tiny Rowland; my wife bought me a biography about this industrialist who was a bit of a maverick back in the 1960s, 1970s and 1980s. That book really excited me, but that was after we had already started our own management consultancy. Even if you look at the early 1990s, there was Richard Branson, and I'm struggling to think of anyone else really. There weren't many people that went out and started companies; there weren't a lot of new ideas appearing in the sort of way they are now.

So, you built up Coffee Nation from a blank sheet of paper. Tell me how you originally came up with the concept.

Well, I had a consulting business at the time which was very successful, but I wanted to do something with a product, and consulting is quite different from that. One of the main drivers was that I wanted to create something that could create revenue while I slept.

How it started was that I read an article in a magazine called *Business Age* about a photocopying company that put photocopiers into newsagents and convenience stores. The attraction to me was their business model. They put the photocopier into a small retailer – the retailer didn't have to buy the machine – then they just split the revenue that was generated by people coming in to use the photocopier machine. The more photocopies that were done, the more revenue that went in the till. The company supplied the signage to go outside that said there was a photocopier available, they supplied the equipment, they maintained it, they supplied the paper and all the consumables. I thought that that was a terrific business model because it would tick all the boxes for me to generate a little bit of revenue from lots of locations and I didn't need to be there.

I think it also appealed because it was less reliant on people versus a people-heavy consulting business. So, that was my original thinking. It wasn't coffee that came first, it was that business model. Then, from there, it was about finding a product that would fit into this revenue-share model. I looked at all sorts of things and had all sorts of ideas. I was thinking about putting something into the thousands of small newsagents in Britain. I couldn't think of what the product would be at first. I thought of travel books, bakery products, toiletries, all sorts of things, and then decided to go and have a look at ideas in America. Often, it seemed that things would start in America and then they'd come to the UK. My wife had some family in Brooklyn, New York, and so I went and stayed with them for a couple of weeks and just got out into Manhattan each day and literally walked the streets, looking for ideas and inspiration.

There were a number of things I saw: one was frozen yogurt, another one was sort of a combination of a restaurant and a cinema. But the weather's not so good here, so I didn't think frozen yogurt would work, and the restaurant and cinema seemed to be very complicated. Then I saw convenience stores (most people know them as 7/11's) and they were selling coffee to take away in a polystyrene cup, selling for a dollar per cup. This was clearly big business for convenience stores. So, I thought, 'Wow, this looks really interesting.

The other thing that stimulated my interest was: on the adjacent corner of the street was a place called Starbucks. I could see that it was a coffee bar, and I was kind of aware that there were one or two coffee bar businesses that were springing up in the UK, and there was a move towards better quality drink and food out of home. So, I thought, 'Coffee could be going somewhere.' But the Starbucks thing to me looked jolly complicated – that was real estate and labour – whereas machines in somebody else's existing business or store seemed much simpler. I thought, 'Great, I'm just taking the store owner's space and I don't need to employ lots of people. This could be another revenue generator for the retailer, bringing in more footfall.' So, that's how it started. Then I came back to the UK to research my idea more fully and write a business plan.

Your entrepreneurial journey wasn't smooth – there were quite a few ups and downs. Tell me more about subsequent years.

So, that was summer 1996. I started off with instant coffee machines mounted on a standalone unit that I had designed. So, this was going to be self-serve instant coffee machine: you take a cup, you put the cup in position and you press the button. At the time, we all drank instant coffee and the idea of having a cappuccino or a caffe latte was that it was a treat, that it was an indulgence. It existed in very, very few places. You knew that if you went to an Italian sandwich bar in London you could get a cappuccino, but this was a fringe, niche product at the time, whereas instant coffee was a British staple.

When I was in America on that initial research visit, I saw a company that supplied these big machines that would grind the beans and steam the milk and then produce the most fabulous coffee. I had a demonstration with this machine, but the problem was it was very, very expensive. It was about $15,000 per machine. So, when I came back to the UK I figured there was no way it was viable, working off the base of what I thought somebody would pay for the coffee. The other side of my thinking was that people drank instant coffee. So what I was doing was putting the instant coffee that they were drinking at home into the shop to take away. So, that's how it started from about mid-1996 to the end of 1997. So, for a good year and a half, I was working jolly hard to prove that this was going to work.

The problem was that I had actually thought, 'What could go wrong?' I was extremely naive, so I made some big mistakes. On the face of it, it just seemed like the photocopier business but with coffee. The reality was that they were very different. One mistake was to assume that what people drank at home, they would want to drink out of home as well. I priced the coffee at around 50 pence and Nescafe convinced me that instant coffee was the way to go. They were very keen on my business model and they liked the idea of getting the Nescafe brand into these non-traditional locations. Not just a jar of coffee on a grocery store shelf, but if they could sell a cup of Nescafe coffee to take away that would be a good way of building their brand. So they agreed to pay for signage for me, which I thought was terrific.

That was the path that I initially went down: instant coffee, 50 pence, branded Nescafe, with powdered milk to make cappuccino or lattes. My thinking was, 'Nobody is going to pay £1 or £1.50 for a cup of coffee in these sorts of locations. It's got to be keenly priced and it's got to be what they drink at home.' The other reason I had to do that was because I couldn't afford these expensive machines that made the real thing with fresh milk. Some of the smaller shop owners liked the idea and I also got trials with some larger convenience store chains. They could see how important a revenue stream takeaway coffee was in the American stores and hoped this could be replicated in Britain. The Spar group liked the idea, so I was trying to prove this in their stores. This excited me because if it worked, I could roll this out into hundreds of locations. I thought, 'Wow this is going to be fairly straightforward. What could be different from the photocopier business?' The problem was that it was very different from the photocopier business. I was trying to convince people to buy something in a place where they'd never bought it before, and the most that we ever sold in any of these locations was around 50 cups a week.

So, 50 cups of coffee at 50 pence a pop – it's not a very exciting revenue stream! The other mistake I made was that alongside that I'd also written a business plan. I thought that was something you were supposed to do, so I'd gone ahead with implementing my business plan. I recruited somebody to be my operations manager to look after the sites and all the logistics with machine deliveries and installations. I was paying him £30,000 a year and he had a company car.

I was doing all of this with the business before I had even proved the concept. I was also trying to raise investment money because I thought this was the thing you were supposed to do. In effect, I was trying to grow a business with a very shaky foundation that didn't have any strong proof or evidence that it would work. So this period went on for about 18 months and it just got harder and harder and I burned through my cash, which had come from my consulting business in agreement with my wife. I'd got an overdraft as well which I burned through and I was £10,000 over the overdraft limit. Eventually, I had to let my ops manager go, which was very difficult and sad because he had worked hard and was very loyal.

So, it was very difficult, but I did keep going because I thought I had to step up and work it out. There were plenty of times where it would have been perfectly acceptable to have accepted defeat. I even remember my wife saying, "Look, nobody can say you haven't given this your best shot." But I knew I would always be asking myself questions, such as, "What if I had just hung in there?" So, it was very difficult and I was hanging on by the skin of my teeth really.

At one point you were technically insolvent. Tell me about that and how you kept going.

Well, there was a eureka moment. I had been out trying to raise money, unsuccessfully. The idea itself was great, but the problem was I'd got the product wrong, I'd got the wrong equipment, I'd got the wrong pricing and I was running around trying to please these retailers rather than actually trying to prove the concept. But fortunately I didn't take any investors' money.

So, by late 1997, I was pretty much in dire straits but my accountants had been very helpful and supportive. Having good advisers by your side from the get-go is very helpful. I was at the point where I couldn't see what the answers were – it was really tough. I wanted to live to fight another day so if I had to wind up the business I was going to do it responsibly and professionally. But I decided to go off on a bit of a round robin tour of some of the machines that I had out there, to see if I could find some answers. I had machines dotted around all sorts of locations; I couldn't be close to them all the time and it was expensive to go and visit them. I jumped in the car and I thought, 'I've just got to give it one last chance.'

This was quite literally my eureka moment. I went to one of the locations and the machine was spotless, probably not because it was kept clean but because very few people were actually using it! I was just about to turn around and walk out when a guy came in. He sort of looked at the machine, and he saw me and asked if I had anything to do with the machine. I said, "Yes it's my business actually." He said, "I think it's a really interesting idea; it's a good idea." Then he said, "But," and my heart sank. He said, "But the problem is I can get exactly what you're selling by just going to the kitchen in my office and making a cup of coffee there. I like the idea of this but if you're going to sell me a cup of coffee in this kind of location, it's got to absolutely knock my socks off. It's got to blow me away." We were in a Spar shop at a petrol station. This doesn't sound like a particularly significant comment, but at that moment that one sentence made me see what I had got wrong.

What I had failed to do was recognize that the business model wasn't going to be what would make people come in to buy the cup of coffee. Customers were not going to be interested in the machine itself. What I had to do was give the customers, the consumer, a fabulous experience. So, I realized in that single moment that what I needed to do was offer exactly what I had turned away from: real gourmet coffee, made fresh with real coffee beans, with steamed and foamed fresh milk. I needed to give them a real coffee bar product. That's how I was going to capture people's attention. To give them something they weren't expecting, knock them off their feet, and really excite them. I immediately realized that rather than trying to push the price down to try and get people to buy the coffee, instead I could actually put the price up.

The other thing I had been trying to do with the instant coffee was convince people to buy it by giving them a free newspaper or sandwich or pastry or whatever. I didn't need any of that now. My realization was that actually if I gave them a fabulous coffee bar product, then I was really doing something different and new and exciting that had never been done before. So I literally turned on the spot, drove back to London and realized all the errors that I had made. Of course, at this point I was almost out of cash. I rang my accountant and said, "I can see the mistake that I've made and where I've gone wrong. Look, I just need to hang on for a little bit longer." Then, because I couldn't afford them, I got in touch with another coffee machine manufacturer and basically blagged my way to borrowing four espresso machines. They were small, table-top machines that would grind the beans and steam the milk. I realized the whole association with Nestle and Nescafe wouldn't work because they were just trying to sell Nescafe.

I went back and got some designs done. This was the first time that the Coffee Nation name appeared. I had designs done for an in-store concession unit that was self-serve with a little coffee machine that ground the beans, steamed the milk, and had Coffee Nation branded cups. So, I got the machines and had an MDF unit built; I was literally running on fumes when it came to money in the bank. To the coffee machine company I said, "Look, I can't pay you now. But if the concept works, then I'll come back and I'll buy the machines from you." I was then able to take out four of the instant coffee machines and replace them with the bean-to-cup machines and pair them with the Coffee Nation branded concession units. I raised the price from 50 pence to around 65 or 70 pence which felt like a huge step and I went from there. What happened was that the sales went from about 50 cups sold per week to perhaps 200 to 300 cups per week. So the jump in revenue was enormous.

Customers were saying, "Wow this is really good." I realized that all my learning until then had delivered me successfully to this point, so I could further refine the concept. I had to do more work with it, but I had got the makings of a new category here. It was that realization that I had a new category that I could own that was so powerful because it gave me confidence. It was off the back of the results from those four machines that I was able to write, for the first time, a business plan that was actually required and I was able to raise £100,000 of seed capital. I also got almost that same amount in a small firms loan that was underwritten by the government.

So what made you decide to write your book? What was the initial catalyst?

I remember my operations director going to an event – I think he saw Simon Woodroffe, the founder of Yo! Sushi, speaking – he came back and said, "You know what? You should write a bloody book because the journey that you went through to get where you're at now is really worth telling." At that point, our revenues were only couple of million or something, this was probably around 2001. He said, "You should do it." And I thought, 'Yeah, yeah I'll get around to it some day.'

My focus at that time was absolutely about owning our category: nail it and scale it, that's what we were about. That was my focus. So, I didn't think any more about the book for many years. It wasn't until after I sold the company in 2008, and actually a couple of years after that where I reconnected with the entrepreneurial world and was thinking about what I was going to do next myself while spending time with other entrepreneurs. A lot of early-stage and larger businesses were coming to me asking for my help, and what I noticed, what I was staggered by, was that lots of people were making all the same kinds of mistakes that I'd made back when I started.

People were sort of creating solutions looking for problems to solve, instead of getting the proof of concept before they tried to build a business. They were writing business plans that were a complete waste of time, as opposed to conserving cash and spending a little to learn a lot. These were all the sorts of mistakes that I'd made. I thought, 'Other people are still doing the same things. I could actually write a book that is in part a how-to guide, no guarantees you're going to succeed, but distilling down the steps to designing a successful business.' We were one of the Top 100 fastest growing companies in the UK for several years running, I'd been named Entrepreneur of the Year by Ernst & Young, and we'd won the Sunday Times/Virgin Atlantic Innovation Award. We'd gone from zero to £20 million in revenue in seven years and making significant profit. It wouldn't have worked out if I hadn't been able to get the original concept right. If I could create a kind of a guide to building a high-growth business, and maximize the odds of success, in what is a high-risk venture, that could really be something. I thought the other part of the book could perhaps be me telling the journey of how we built Coffee Nation and how we did it. I thought that would be of interest and I could give some learning points along the way.

I think the other thing that motivated me was the explosion of interest in entrepreneurship in the UK, which is fantastic. But there's a bit of a fallacy: you watch programmes on the TV like *The Apprentice* or *Dragons' Den* and there is this kind of perception that you can pretty quickly get to be really successful and make a lot of money. The music industry and the media further propagate that. I just thought, 'That's bullshit.' It takes real guts and courage. You've got to be prepared to look yourself in the mirror and be prepared to change and to listen to people that can help you. You've got to have something worthwhile because plenty of business ideas are just never going to fly; they're just not worth it, there's no demand. It's a bit like me and my cups of instant coffee – it wasn't exciting. So, I thought, 'I've got to tell the real story and not just some fantasy that anyone can do it, but to tell the truth about what it's really like.'

The other thing was then to try to also focus not just on the startup journey but what would come next. That was the thinking: if we can get more startups surviving and becoming higher growth businesses, then that could really help the economy because it's high-growth businesses that contribute more than half the jobs created in the UK. It's no longer the major corporations; it's mid-market growth companies. So, if we can increase the odds of more startups getting to the next stage and becoming mid-market companies, with revenues of £10 million and beyond, creating profitability and jobs, they are going to be the engines of the country going forward.

So, it was a combination of things. I thought, 'I've got a good reputation. I've got credibility. I've got a track record. I think it's a worthwhile thing that I could put back into the community.' So, that's how it came about.

How did you find the experience of writing your book? Did it come easily to you?

I started off by writing down the journey of building Coffee Nation into sort of bite-sized chunks, chronologically, and then the how-to guide part of the book. I took each element of the idea – entrepreneur, marketplace, business model, etc. – with main headings and all the things you really had to get right. So that was the rough blueprint.

The book got published at the end of 2013; it was around the beginning of 2012 that I started writing it. I didn't do this every day. I did it over a period of 18 months or so. I'd kept all my notebooks from when we were building the company in from 1996 onwards and all the board papers (we literally had a board meeting every month for about 12 years). I pieced it all together and it was still very strong in my mind. There are times when it would really flow, and once I got into the flow it was usually quite enjoyable.

It would typically be that I'd get my head down and crack out perhaps a few pages or a chunk or section and that would take anything from a few hours to a couple days of solid work. It just gradually came together and I'd ask my wife or daughter to read it. It probably took about 18 months overall.

You've been very candid about the highs and lows of your journey in the book. Did you feel comfortable about sharing your mistakes with everyone else? Or did you feel a temptation to tidy it up?

No, not at all. Because it's a hell of a ride starting and building a company and the odds of failing are very high. Very, very few make it. So, that was the whole purpose – to be honest and truthful. We made tons of mistakes. In the early days, they were all my mistakes and that was the point when I learned about being honest. Hopefully I can help other people avoid the same mistakes.

You're published by Harriman House. Tell me a little about that.

Well, there were a couple of publishers, one or two, who wanted to publish my book, which was fabulous. I think what appealed to me about Harriman House was that I was talking directly to the MD – I liked that relationship. Also, they liked the format of the book as opposed to wanting to make any significant changes. I think the other publishers wanted me to modify the format. My concern with that was having to think in a different way: I felt that I'd got a pretty good idea of the format and I thought my format could work.

I think Harriman House really liked the style of the book and they were very easy to deal with. So it was about being true to what my purpose was with the book, and telling the story as it really was and so on. I thought that might have gotten lost with the other publishers or that they didn't really see that. So, it was just easy to work with Harriman House; I thought that the guy who worked with me on the editing was great.

And when the book came out, tell me a little about what you did to launch it and to sell it.

We did a book launch event and got some press coverage. I wrote some short excerpts on elements of things around starting and growing a business, whether it was a piece about the founder, or proving the idea or whatever it might be, and those went online and into business magazines, websites, etc. There was coverage in national press, and there was business press coverage, such as *Management Today*, for example. Most of that was coordinated by Harriman House, and there were quite a few speaker events that came off the back of that. So, we did quite well.

You've been featured in quite a few papers and magazines. Can you share any tips for new authors for getting the most out of a media interview, particularly with regard to promoting a book?

In terms of books it's about having a clear message. We were in the media quite a lot when we were building the company and I think then it was the same as having the book. It was about having a clear message that gives the journalist a hook to hang their hat on.

So, the message when we were building the company was: we have created this new category of self-serve gourmet coffee and we're putting fabulous coffee bar products wherever people are, 24/7. Nobody's done it before and this is how we do it. And, with the book it was: a story about how to build a high-growth business in the UK. This was by now a well-known brand and I think we had sold about 100 million cups of coffee by the time the book came out, and the book was about how we did it. It is a genuine, real, truthful account which is going to be of interest to other early-stage entrepreneurs, and the other side of it is the how-to guide for increasing your chances of being in a high-growth scenario rather than a survival scenario. It appealed to journalists and we got some decent coverage.

Do you take much notice of your reviews and the feedback you're getting for your book on Amazon?

It's nice to see, of course it is. It just validates the fact that it has fulfilled its purpose. I get lots of people who say to me, "I've read your book and found it really helpful, thank you. It saved me money, saved me time" or "I quit and started something different as I realised I was flogging a dead horse." Or they say, "It helped me turn a corner" or "It helped me work more on the idea first" or "It's helped me not rush back into something after I've sold." So I get a lot of people who talk about the book and it seems to have been very well received.

What sort of impact has the book had on your personal and professional life?

I think it's been a nice thing to do, it's drawn a nice line to say: that was quite an achievement. Of course, the company's been sold again. It's called Costa Express and there's been two exits. It's been a staple of British convenience stores and supermarkets for many years and now in many countries overseas as well. So, that's fantastic and to encapsulate it in the book is a really nice feeling. I think that it's certainly underpinned my work now as a mentor for other entrepreneurs.

After I sold the business, I was starting to get asked by CEOs and founders of companies, typically in that mid-market tier, perhaps £5 to £10 million and upwards businesses, to help and have a look at their company if they were struggling or wondering, 'What next?' At first, I thought I wanted to do it all over again, but I gradually realized that I enjoyed helping others and I didn't want to start another business. I think the book has been useful because I know some of the people in companies I'm working with now have read my book and they've commented to me, "It's fabulous, because we know you really did do it. You went through all this shit and all the dark times – and this isn't glamorous, but this is what it really is like and what it takes." So I think it's been really quite useful in that regard.

Summary for Super-Busy Entrepreneurs

- Write a book to document the journey you've travelled to get where you are now.

- You may notice a lot of people asking for your help and making all the same kinds of mistakes that you made when you started out. This confirms that you have a book idea that will be of value to others.

- Consider writing a book that is part how-to guide, and part telling your own story giving some learning points along the way.

- Think of a common fallacy or misconception in your niche. Consider writing a book that tells the truth about what it's really like.

- Write a book that has a bigger mission, so that it changes the world in a positive way. For example, improving the economy and creating new jobs.

- Break down your story into bite-sized chunks, chronologically. Take each element of the idea and give it a heading. List all the things you really have to get right to give you a rough blueprint.

- Use your notebooks and board papers from over the years to jog your memory, especially if you're including autobiographical information.

- Resist the temptation to tidy up the highs and lows of your journey. Be honest and truthful to help other people avoid the same mistakes.

- Don't say, "Yes," to the first publisher who likes your book. Choose a publisher who is in alignment with your goals and values.

- Choose a publisher who likes the existing format of your book, rather than wanting you to make significant changes.
- With your book launch, be prepared to write some short excerpts on elements in your book to go in business magazines, websites, etc. Also, be prepared for promotional speaker events.
- To get the most out of your media interviews, have a very clear message so that it gives the journalist a clear story that will be of interest to their readership.
- A book is a good way to draw a line under your achievements. A book that shows how you overcame the really challenging times in your life is great for inspiring and motivating others.

LUCA LONGOBARDI

*"I started to write this book right after I
came out of jail ... to express all my anger and
sadness."*

Luca Longobardi is an Italian entrepreneur and former venture
capitalist who founded his own investment banking group, State
Capital, in 1999. This grew into a multi-national company managing
and overseeing deals worth billions.

He gained notoriety for being wrongfully accused of laundering
money for the Italian mafia and was held for a month in a maximum-
security prison in Brazil. He was eventually cleared of all charges,
but it was too late to save his business. When he was released, he
discovered that everything he'd built had fallen apart.

He has since opened 108 Garage in Notting Hill, which has been acclaimed as one of London's finest restaurants.

His first self-published book, *Branded 'The Mafia's Banker'* (2015) documented his time in jail. A YouTube video promoting the book went viral and received over 1.5 million views, and the book has sold over 250,000 copies.

I first published my book on Amazon. I had initial proposals from a couple of publishing companies, but then at the end I decided to go solo, which is part of my life in everything I do because I'm a self-taught entrepreneur. So I said, "I'm going to try my first book with a self-publishing approach to see how this works." With a friend of mine, who is a producer and film director, I made a short video of around four minutes and it went viral. The video was really, really well made and it received more than a million hits and that helped me to sell the book.

Actually, I was not interested in the financial outcome. I was mostly interested in spreading the message and in regaining some dignity out of the story. Money was not my main issue, so I said, "If I sell one book or I sell 100, it doesn't make any difference for me. The important thing is the result, and people will know exactly what happened." At the end, I've been pleased with the results.

Your video promoting your book won the Best Trailer/Promos award at the Los Angeles Independent Film Festival, and your film *An*

Italian Food Story **won the Best Inspirational Film award at the Los Angeles Film Awards didn't it?**

The video is *Branded: 'The Mafia's Banker'*. It had a lot of views on YouTube when it was first published. But then it was re-edited again because there were a couple of mistakes in the video, and so we took down the video, and we republished it. So the real hits would be over 1.5 million on that video. I really like this video. It's really helped with making movie proposals to production companies. Every time that I show it to a director or a producer, or even a few actors that I've been in touch with lately, everybody's really, really impressed.

It won several awards, like Los Angeles Film Festival. It's gone viral because people like it. That has helped me to get the results with my book.

And you sold 250,000 books off the back of this video.

Yes, lots of digital copies because my book was published as a Kindle edition, and lots of paperbacks. A lot of paperbacks were sold in Italy because digital books are not massive there. In the UK, I sold a lot of paperbacks; also US, a lot of paperbacks. So between the two, paperback and digital, I sold 250,000 copies.

How do sales in your home country, Italy, compare to the sales globally?

Well, I'd say that probably they were worth 30 per cent of the total. I had sales in Australia and Canada, a little bit in Germany. I also have a proposal from a Brazilian publishing company to publish the book in Brazil with them, which I'm considering. We have plans to launch new books – I have a new version of my first book, which will be double the size.

My first book was a prison story mostly; it's not the entire story of my life in every single aspect. So the new version of the book will be closer to the movie than to the first version of my book. It will be much more sophisticated, much more intense, and give much more detail about how I started out and took every single step.

You didn't find writing your book easy. Tell me about how you managed to get your words down on the page.

Well, this was probably the hardest part because I've never been a good writer, not even in essays at school. I was a bad student and I have A.D.D., so for me, writing an essay was a nightmare. I started to write this book right after I came out of jail, and it was a way to just express all my anger and sadness at what happened. The first version took me seven or eight months because I was writing as I was travelling in my spare time. So the first version of the book was a disaster in my opinion, as I look at it today.

It was really everything that a writer shouldn't do: expressing all the anger, all the sadness and remorse. I wanted to kill the whole world at that time. As I was starting to forgive and cool down and begin a new journey, I was modifying paragraphs and re-touching it. Then I completely let it go because at one point my wife did not agree with publishing this book because she was concerned about increasing our exposure again. My family had been exposed to the media already, and launching this book felt like bringing back everything from the past. We didn't need that. So I kind of put it aside for some time.

Then in around 2014, we got separated. I moved to London and decided that I wanted to finish the book and publish it. I picked up the old material; I went through, and I thought, "Oh my God, that's not me completely. That wasn't me before, and it's not me now; that is me in the transition." So I decided that I was not going to take anything of the material that I had written before. I decided to go on a new journey and write a new book.

I took almost nine months' sabbatical, travelling a little bit through Italy and through England and some other places. I decided to begin a journey in the restaurant business as a new beginning. Basically, I wanted to reinvent myself. As I was travelling, I began to write my memories again. This was a completely different approach to what I had written before, and what was apparent to me before. I discovered sides of myself and of my life that I would never have been able to do without starting a different life.

So I wrote this new book, which hasn't been easy, but I followed a certain procedure while I was travelling through Italy and other parts of Europe. It was so much easier this time to write about what I was thinking about my life and what I was thinking about the past and what happened to me. So it has been tough in a way, but much easier than it was in the past.

Were you disciplined about giving yourself an hour a day or did you write only when you felt like doing it?

I use my laptop to write when I'm travelling, and sometimes I use my iPhone to open the notes and write paragraphs. In the beginning, I thought that the best way to write a book was to be inspired and write only when you feel like it. Instead, I ended up understanding that to write a book you have to follow a procedure just as you do in your area of discipline. You have to wake up at a certain time; you decide that at that time you are going to write for two hours, and then in the afternoon you're going to write for another two hours if you have a job in the middle. Or, if you are a full-time author, you should write from 8 o'clock in the morning till 12 o'clock, take a pause, and then write again in the afternoon.

So I was travelling, and I was visiting food companies, and so I wrote in between. I built that discipline in writing, which was mostly in the morning and in the afternoon or at night. That's the only way that I think you can write a book that is consistent and you finish it. Think about what would happen if you are inspired one day and then you start to write a page, and you just think of 2,000 other things to say. Or suppose you say, "I'm not inspired today," and you know very well it will take five years to write it in that way. So if you want to write a book, and you want to publish it in six months, a year, you should definitely have discipline.

Marketing a book is also essential to its success isn't it? Your Gumtree video had over 300,000 views in the week it was launched.

Yes – the Gumtree video happened when I was opening the restaurant, and I put an ad on Gumtree to find a chef. The chef that I have originally answered the ad on Gumtree. Now, the restaurant has become one of London's most acclaimed restaurants, and the question from everybody is, "How did you guys find each other?" And the answer was: Gumtree.

So there was an article in *The Times* a few months ago that was about how the chef found his Mafia banker on Gumtree. So the CEO of Gumtree picked up the phone and called me at the restaurant. He originally left a message, as I wasn't there. I went back to the restaurant and the hostess told me, "A guy from Gumtree called you, left this number, and if you can return his call, he wanted to talk to you about something." I thought that it was something about placing an advertisement. I use Gumtree a lot, so usually, they call you to arrange to give you some offer or some special price.

So I didn't even call back for over a week. Then I picked up the phone, I had the number one day, and I said, "Let me call this for our launch. Gumtree will probably make a special offer or a free offer or something." So I called them up, and a secretary picked up the phone and said, "I'll give you the CEO of Gumtree," and I spoke with him. He said, "I've read great things about the restaurant. I loved the article in *The Times*, and I loved the story. We're launching a new advertising campaign. We're looking to scale in a different market also, and we would like to use your video as a testimonial. So I have everything set up – if you agree, we can shoot this video in the next couple of weeks."

So I was back and forth organising this video. I didn't want it to just be an advert for Gumtree. I wanted it to be something in which we expressed a message of hope for people: if you open a restaurant, you don't have to go and hire a big-time chef to become a top restaurant in London or anywhere in the world. Actually, with some effort, passion, and creativity, you can end up being like us. I'm an ex-banker turned into a restaurateur. I put some effort and courage and passion into something completely new, and that was the message. So they came and shot this video in one day, and we had really good feedback. We've had lots of hits already on Facebook and on their Gumtree pages and on their media channel.

So what kind of impact has your first book had on your life and your business?

The book has completely changed my life I would say, because before I was a guy that had a successful life, and at one point my life vanished completely – immediately, in 24 hours, I lost everything. I lost a reputation and everything else, right? And so that was how I was still perceived in all the years prior to writing the book; I was hiding myself almost. I didn't want anybody to Google my name, I didn't want to show up anywhere. I didn't even give out my business card because I didn't want anybody to get my name, go and Google and find out that I was defined and branded as "the Mafia's banker". I was branded not just by the media, but by Google too.

So writing the book for me was finally coming out with the real story of who I really was. I was actually putting myself, my face, on the street again. I was finding the courage to fight back … accepting whatever people were thinking about me, whatever everybody was naming me, and making it part of me and part of my life. I could not avoid it any more. I could not be scared of it, I could not be ashamed of it, and I could not be hiding from it, so I made it part of me. So writing the book made me probably more truthful than I was before. Now, I am able to say, "Yes, you can Google me, and yes, they call me the Mafia's banker. The story is this one: yes, I am that guy."

So it gave me a new face and a way of facing people of all kinds, who I had been avoiding in my business and personal life. I had become at one point almost introverted, which I'm not in my relationships. I am a guy that talks a lot, but in the six years prior to writing the book, I found myself in a spot where I was not communicating as I used to do. It gave

216

me a new life, a new beginning, because today I meet some people, and the first thing that they say is, "Oh, how did you get the restaurant?" So I've got to tell them the whole story, because it's obvious I've never had a restaurant before in my life.

They will ask, "What did you do before?"

"I was a banker."

"Why did you leave the banking business?"

I cannot say that I sold the business, and I cannot say I shut down the business. So I tell them, "I was forced into leaving the banking business."

Then more questions come, and I share my story. The perception of everybody is, "Oh my God, this is an incredible story – unbelievable."

I think that being a banker makes you a boring person. In the world of today, nobody wants to deal or sit down with a banker. You are boring. So I think who I am today makes me a more interesting person, even to myself because I am having to ask myself all the time: where was I and how did I get to be where I am right now? Who am I going to be in the future?"

So for me, it was a little bit like regaining my dignity. This has nothing to do with ego. I had a discussion some time ago with my girlfriend. She asked, "Why do you want to regain your face?" It's not about regaining face. You've got to understand that in 40 years, I may have met 2,000 people, 10,000 or 100,000 people – it doesn't matter. But there are people that knew me when I was 12, 13, 14 years old, and they know me as a good guy, who's grown up in a good family, an honest family. Suddenly, these people that knew me back then, they start to hear from the newspapers that I was involved with the Mafia. I was called "the Mafia's banker", so I was a bad guy. So it's not that I want to look good, it's about 40 years of history with people that care about me, or who may have just crossed paths with me during my life. You build a story of your life over the years, and you want to leave a good story about you.

Of course you care about what other people think. It's bullshit whenever someone says, "I don't care, I don't give a shit what's said about me," because it's not true. You care about what other people think because you care about doing good, and if you care about doing good it's because you want to leave a good memory of yourself to whoever you love... And to do that, you've got to be able to have confidence to trust yourself, and eventually to have dignity. To do that, you need a certain kind of dignity, and I lost it for some time when all this happened because somebody stripped that away from me.

Even though I know inside that I went to jail as an honest man, I don't want to appear as the good guy that went to jail. I was a banker. So being a banker, you can't be a banker and be honest. It doesn't match. They don't fit together, the two things, because being in the banking business you abide by certain rules, certain guidelines. They are given to you by the top-level management of the banking business, which tell you to follow them. If you have to sell some security or a certain kind of government bond because the bank has a certain number of those bonds, a certain quantity of those securities, and they've got to get rid of it, you have to sell it. If you work in the banking business, you will know why they are going to do it because it's their interest in that moment, even if it's not a good thing for the third party that will buy those securities. So you work on the edge all the time of what is good and what is bad, what is honest and dishonest, what is legal and illegal. At this stage, I was running after the compelling attractiveness or charm that can inspire devotion in others: charisma. Today, I try to fix the true me, the source of my inspiration, influence, and leadership rather than simply trying to mask it: character.

So if you are out to do big business in banking, you're walking on a knife edge, and that edge has dangers, and at any point can have consequences. So I coped with that, and I accepted that. I wanted to be big and make more money, so you have to walk on the limits. Sometimes you are lucky, and nothing happens to you – most people are lucky – and sometimes God just takes it away from you. If this happens, it is your time to fall and to understand exactly who you are and what you are going to do in life in the future.

But anyway, even that walking on the edge, I mean, I still believe that I am an honest person in terms of mindset, and how I think. Going to prison, you are living your life, but you are also looking behind at your life that you have built in the past 40 years, and you are also looking into the future at which way you are going to live in the next 40 years. Because going to prison makes you a completely different man. It means you will get stripped of your dignity because you're going to prison, which makes you automatically seem like a bad man for 99 per cent of the world out there. Life is different when you are in and when you are out. There is time to think about who you were and who you are going to be and who you are at that time. So for me, writing the book was trying to understand myself and recoup my dignity and what type of man I was.

Your ex-wife was originally opposed to you writing the book because she felt you were writing about your personal life and revisiting the past. What were your own feelings while you were writing it?

I was divorced and separated by the time I wrote it, so I was not worried any more what my wife would think. It was my call, and I wanted to do it. And yes, when I launched the title, there was an internal conflict over what I was going to call it. If I put 'Mafia' somewhere in the title, I felt I was going to expose myself even more. And then I was speaking with a friend of mine, and she said, "I think you should call it exactly what they call you. You know, they call you 'the Mafia's banker'. You should call it exactly how it was. It would be controversial, a strong title." So I decided that was what I was going to call it.

I think that the day that I launched my book, I set myself free. It felt like a different moment; I felt like a different man. It was almost like losing all the weight of seven years that I had inside me. It was incredible, it was like getting my freedom back again.

Before launching the book, oh my God, it was a nightmare every time that I would hear the word 'Mafia' tied to my name. At that time, you would look along the bar on the Internet, and Google would auto complete my name automatically with 'the Mafia's banker'. You would read lots of information on Google, which I have since asked to be removed. So 70 per cent of what was written on Google I contacted the sources directly and asked for the information to be removed. Now when you write Luca Longobardi and my name comes up and you find the book.

So it's allowed you to reclaim your life and reframe everything that happened?

Absolutely, absolutely. I'm not ashamed any more. All this to regain my dignity has brought me a lot of exposure, and my restaurant has become very successful. I'm opening another restaurant, then re-publishing the book, and then writing another book and working on the movie, and I also receive a lot of speaking engagements now. I'm pretty busy.

You cannot really control it, and it's difficult to refuse because I'm at a stage of my life where I like to be helpful to other people who relate to a story like mine or people that want to build a story like mine: being a guy aged 21 who left Italy with no money and made millions, then lost everything and reinvented himself again. You can make everything back again in terms of success, you can reinvent yourself. There is always an opportunity to put passion somewhere and to make it work.

Tell me more about your new books and your plans for them.

Well, we have another two coming, right? One is *Not a Cookbook,* which is a little bit of my story through food. I have always had this big passion for food since I was young, and I learned this at home with my family, my mother, my father. Since I was a 12-year-old guy, I was looking at my mother cooking, and the passion was growing. Then I moved to New York with no money, and this became a street food time of my life. With no money, you eat like a dog on very cheap stuff.

Then, there was the time when I started to make money, and I was making the transition from making no money to a little bit of money. So I invited women home in order to save money, and I was cooking for them, which developed my relationship with food, by testing food and cooking food. And then there was the time when I had a lot of money, and I went through the whole process of understanding sophisticated cuisine.

Then, came the restaurant. There is the life of the chef and the whole period of his life becoming a chef, how we opened the restaurant together and how this happened, and lots of recipes during this chapter. So we called this *Not a Cookbook* because it's not a cookbook, but there are recipes inside. There is a little bit of a cookbook, there is a little bit of drama, there is a little bit of fun, and there is a little bit of entrepreneurship. This is the book we're launching now.

After that, I have my first book to release again. It is the complete book that I have already written basically, with some more spicy stories added about some of the events of my life. Some of the stuff I had already written I have deleted because the first one was perhaps more a diary than a book. This one is partly an autobiography and partly a motivational book. In my first book, the autobiography, that was for people to understand a little bit about me, and I was helping myself with that book. With this second one, I'm going to try to help others – I want to help them to understand themselves and to motivate themselves.

So you're wanting to help and inspire others. You have quite a few high-profile speaking engagements off the back of your book too.

I'm scheduled for a TED speaking event in December, and I have a company engagement. I also have one in Spain in September with lastminute.com, the online travel group, which is an event with all the employees they have around the world. And then I have a couple of others.

You also have a movie in production off the back of your book. What stage is that at now?

So as you know, a movie is something which goes up and down, up and down, up and down in terms of production. Everybody seems to have an interest, and then you have to develop the screenplay and then the production. Since I wrote the book, I received a lot of calls from big movie producers to sign for option rights: "You're selling the option, and we'll do whatever we want." I was not interested in this. Most of these offers I refused as I don't give a shit about the money – I want my story to be out and to be told right. I'm not going to sign away the option rights, I want to participate in the message because that's what I'm interested in.

I had other producers coming forward with better terms, so I am at the stage right now of deciding between three production companies. I am in the process of deciding which one I will choose to begin the whole journey with the screenplay. In the next month, I will sign with one of the three proposals that I have. From there, I will develop a screenplay with the scriptwriter which will take me probably three or four months spending time together a couple of days a week, going through my life again in every single detail. And then we will go through the process of production.

I'd like to be able to participate in this, even if I can't do it full-time because I'm busy. I am launching a new restaurant right now, which is opening in September. It's going to be a bigger restaurant than the one that I opened, and then right after this one, I'm getting involved in a hospitality project which is more sophisticated. It's like a hotel, combined with flats. It's a building with 20 apartments with a flat-hotel upstairs and a restaurant and clubhouse. I'm an entrepreneur, and that's what makes me excited, so I don't want to be full-time producing a movie. It's not me, it's not what I do in life. I don't wish to be the main actor of my movie, so

I said, "No" to that. But I'd definitely like a cameo role somewhere – 30 seconds, a minute, whatever – it'll be something like that.

And what do your daughters think about all this?

I have two daughters, Raffaella, 12, and Julia, 16: they are living in Milan with my ex-wife. They didn't know anything about what happened until I launched the book. So two months prior to launching the book, it was Christmas time. We were in London walking, and I told them the story, and their reaction was unexpected because they were so interested, and they kept asking questions. Kids are so intrigued by: "What is it like in prison?" "What have you done?" "What do you do in prison?" "Who did you meet in prison?"

So it was really an interesting and pleasant conversation. They kept asking me at night and over the following days about the prison story, which made them more familiar with everything that happened. I believe that they are proud of who I am. They were proud before, and now actually this has made them even prouder because kids are attached to everything that is entertainment in their lives. So they know that I have a movie going on, they know that I am speaking at events. Lately, they went with their mum to Tuscany, and they were in a hotel. They were taking some cooking classes, and somebody asked, "Oh, what does your father do?"

"Oh, my father lives in London."

"Ah, really, London?"

So it came up, "My father wrote a book."

"Oh, what did he write a book about?"

"It's called *Branded 'The Mafia's Banker'*. He was not in the Mafia, he wrote a book because…" They told everyone about the story, and everyone bought the book at the end of the cooking class. So my daughters like it. Julia, she wants to be a singer, and she sings already. Raffaella wants to be an actress, so she tells me all the time, "I'm going to act in your movie. I have to act in your movie."

Summary For Super-Busy Entrepreneurs

- Produce both a digital and paperback version of your book to cover all global markets.
- Use a book to set the record straight if there has been a misconception, misunderstanding, or miscarriage of justice.
- Make a high-quality video of around three minutes to promote your book. Test out people's reactions. Aim for it to go viral.
- Use your book and promotional video to pitch movie proposals to film producers and directors.
- Don't be afraid to revise, rewrite and relaunch your book if you feel you have left out vital parts of the story.
- You can write a book even if you hated writing essays at school.
- Take a disciplined and business-like approach to writing your book. Write for a set period of time each day; write even if you don't feel inspired.
- Use your laptop or iPhone to help you write while you're travelling and away from your desk.
- YouTube is a great platform to promote your book. But also consider less obvious options such as Gumtree.
- Writing a book can help with your SEO when people search for you on Google.
- A book can help you regain your identity and dignity if your reputation has been tarnished. It also can enable you to reframe and embrace parts of your life you may feel ashamed of.
- Your family is likely to have different reactions to your book. They may feel exposed if you are writing about your personal life. Or they may find it exciting and something to be proud of.

- Use your book to help others and provide a roadmap for those who want to follow in your footsteps.
- Consider mixing genres: an autobiography combined with a motivational business book, or a cookery book combined with an entrepreneurial book.
- Use your book to help you secure high-profile speaking engagements such as TED talks or corporate conferences.
- Beware of signing away your rights completely when negotiating the film or TV option for your book.
- You may not want a career as an actor, but consider a walk-on part if you're lucky enough to secure a film deal.
- Use your book to share your story with your children, and reveal parts of your life story they may not know about.
- A book can help grow your business, even if the topic is not directly related.

Acknowledgements

I almost didn't write this book.

But then an airmail envelope dropped through my letterbox with the first chapter in it from my friend, Dan S Kennedy. He'd casually mentioned that he wanted to be included in my next book. I thought he was being polite and would soon forget about it. But no, true to his word, he'd diligently written his chapter.

A family tragedy had pulled the carpet out from under my feet. But the gentle nudge gave me the encouragement I needed to get back up and to set to work on this book. Thank you, Dan.

I'm fortunate to be one of those people who love what they do. You might call me a workaholic, but for me, it's a privilege to do what I do for a living. From an early age, I always had my head in a book and loved to learn new things. That hasn't changed, except that now I don't have to read books with a torch under the bedcovers, and I don't get scolded for it!

I am blessed to have some very special people in my business and my personal life.

Firstly, a massive thank you to everyone, including friends and clients, who have generously given their time and expertise to help with compiling this book.

I have some real diamonds in my team, people who regularly go the extra mile for me, and that is an understatement. So a humungous thank you to: Marina McCarron for critical feedback, Brian Cross for proof-reading, Ella Gascoigne for PR and Vikiana for book cover design.

Thanks to my sister, Chloe, who has always been there for me during the rollercoaster ride of our life. Also, to my brother-in-law, David, who is skilled with the garden shears and electric drill and is kind enough to share those talents!

Thanks so much to my grandparents, who looked after us in their home for many years and taught us the importance of honesty, integrity, and helping others. They were never afraid to "do different" and ignore the naysayers, and encouraged us to do the same. We took so many of the wonderful things they did for granted, as all children do, but those years were oh so precious.

Thanks to my partner, Chris, for being so laid back and for tolerating many hours spent at my desk, either reading other entrepreneurs' books or writing my own.

The biggest thank you goes to my three amazing children, Cormac, Tierni, and Chiara. You shine your light on the world, each and every day. I love you and couldn't have done a page of this without you.

Afterword

Earlier on in this book, I mentioned the owner of a film production company who announced he would write his book before the next session of a business networking event. That was six weeks ago.

Today, as I finish re-reading this manuscript and prepare to send it off to the proof-reader, an email popped up in my mailbox:

My business partner and I were at your talk on How to Write a Book. You might remember Dan announcing that by the next meeting we would have written our book!

I just wanted to get in touch because we've actually more or less finished our book now.

True to his word, the first draft is finished. He's dared to put himself on the line, to make himself vulnerable, to open himself up to criticism. No doubt, the critics will be saying: "But is it any good?"

The jury is out until I read it. But Dan has achieved what so many others dream of, but fail to achieve. He's a doer, not a dreamer.

Which one are you?

OTHER BOOKS BY STEPHANIE J HALE

Millionaire Women, Millionaire You

Tips from women multi-millionaires
who overcame incredible hurdles.

Contributors include: Gill Fielding (*Secret Millionaire/The Apprentice*); Barbara Corcoran (*Shark Tank*); Rachel Elnaugh (*Dragons' Den*); Linda Franklin (*The Real Cougar Woman*).

Celebrity Authors' Secrets

Tips from famous authors who were once unknown.

Contributors include: Jeffrey Archer (*Not a Penny More, Not a Penny Less*); Barbara Taylor Bradford (*A Woman of Substance*); John Gray (*Men Are from Mars*); Eric Carle (*The Very Hungry Caterpillar*); Anne Rice (*Interview with the Vampire*); Terry Pratchett (*Discworld*); Bernard Cornwell (*Sharpe*); Joanne Harris (*Chocolat*); James Redfield (*The Celestine Prophecy*).

How to Hook a Literary Agent

Discover the pros and cons of having a literary agent. Learn how to write an enticing pitch that will stand out from the thousands of others.

Available on Amazon

IS YOUR BOOK IDEA STRONG ENOUGH?

If you'd like frank and honest feedback about your own book idea and how to get published, do feel free to get in touch via email and I'll be happy to help.

I look forward to hearing from you at:
oxfordwriters@me.com

www.oxfordwriters.com

9 780992 846084